# TOWARDS A BETTER UNDERSTANDING:
## Aspects of Mental Handicap

Robert Senior

# TOWARDS A BETTER UNDERSTANDING:
## Aspects of Mental Handicap

**Robert Senior**

Euromonitor Publications Limited
87-88 Turnmill Street, London EC1M 5QU

First edition 1985

Robert Senior

Published by
Euromonitor Publications Limited
87-88 Turnmill Street
London EC1M 5QU

Telephone: 01-251 8024



ISBN: 0 86338 075 1

**British Library Cataloguing in Publication Data**

Senior, Robert
Towards a better understanding : aspects of mental handicap.
1. Mental retardation
I. Title
616.85'88 RC570

ISBN 0-86338-075-1

Cover design by Rhiannon Saunders-Davies

Phototypeset by Photoprint, 9-11 Alexandra Lane, Torquay
Printed and bound in Great Britain by Woolnough Bookbinding

# CONTENTS

# FOREWORD

Many books have been written about mental handicap in our society but few are books that you or I might read. They are cluttered with medical and sociological jargon and do not even approach the doubts and questions innermost in our minds, minds filled with misunderstandings and often real fears about mental handicap and our mentally handicapped population. This book attempts to shed light on this difficult, complex subject by presenting a broad guide to some of the fundamental aspects of mental handicap and the treatment of the mentally handicapped by society. It would not have been possible if I had not met mentally handicapped people, and it is on their behalf that I have written it.

Other people helped to put this little book together, and my thanks go to Gay Pratt, Gerda Jones, Georgina Westbrook, John Gregg, Gill Saxon and Mary Holland of Mencap, and the other organisations featured in the book.

*Robert Senior, 1984*

*The cover shows Nina Weill who played Nina in the television series 'Crossroads'. Photo courtesy Central TV.*

## William in the womb

Did Charles and Diana consider the possibility of aborting the foetus who is now Prince William? There is one, admittedly slender, piece of evidence that they did. The typed official announcement of the birth of their son had the time of his arrival written in by hand. This suggests—as the newspapers long ago suggested—that the Palace knew the sex of the baby before it knew the time of his arrival. Conceivably it prepared two 'official announcements' and issued the relevant one when the time was known. But it is also possible that Princess Diana had had amniocentesis earlier in her pregnancy to test for Down's syndrome (mongolism). In this test, fluid surrounding the foetus in the womb is drawn off via a needle through the abdomen and analysed. In the course of this analysis, the sex of the baby would also have been revealed.

There are two points about this test. First, there is no point in doing it unless the woman is prepared for termination if it reveals an abnormality. Second, there is a small risk (between 1 and 2 per cent) that the procedure will initiate a spontaneous abortion, and there is also a very small risk of the needle damaging the foetus or placenta. For these reasons, and because of the cost, the Royal College of Obstetricians and Gynaecologists recommends that the test should not be carried out on women under 35 because only over that age does the risk of bearing a mongol child become 'significant'. But naturally the significance of a risk depends on who you are.

*New Society,* 1982

CHAPTER ONE

# UNDERSTANDING MENTAL HANDICAP

'Mentally handicapped' is the most common term used in Great Britain to describe a section of the public who possess a lower than average level of intelligence. Their handicap is like any other permanent disability, such as someone who is physically handicapped through the loss of a limb. And like any type of physical handicap, it is incurable. Around 1.25 million people in Great Britain suffer from mental handicap, over 2% of the total population, one in every 45 people.

A person who is mentally handicapped is just as much a member of society as anyone else and, like anyone who possesses a disability or impairment, is entitled not only to the same rights and services as society as a whole, but also to special needs and facilities which Britain, as a relatively affluent nation, should be able to provide for the care of disadvantaged people.

The mentally handicapped are part of our disabled community. Around 10% of the entire British population are disabled in some way or another, of which 20-25% are mentally handicapped. Some people are both mentally and physically handicapped, and many mentally handicapped people are less physically able than people with a higher intelligence because of the mental involvement in the physical actions of the human body.

More severely handicapped people often suffer from physical as well as mental disabilities. The most common related physical disabilities are spasticity, epilepsy, blindness, hearing defects and heart problems. Their life expectancy may be less than the national average, and they may be more susceptible to illness and disease.

But people who are mentally handicapped are not, in any sense, ill.

They have an incurable handicap which will remain with them for the duration of their lives. A person who is mentally ill has a temporary ailment, a condition brought about by emotional stress. By a visit to a doctor, a psychiatrist, or even through a programme of counselling and guidance, mental illnesses can be cured, and almost always are. It is the difference between breaking your leg, and losing it.

Mental handicap is a disability which a person will live with all their lives. It may mean that the mentally handicapped child will be dependent on other people, including its parents, more than the average child. It may mean that the mentally handicapped child will require special educational needs in order that its full potential be realised, extending to the teaching of social as well as academic skills. It may mean that the mentally handicapped adult will not be able to engage in as productive a job as an adult with a higher level of intelligence. However, in many instances this is not the case, and mentally handicapped people move through lives with the same degree of fulfilment as anyone else. And even if it were, there are no grounds to suppose that a person with mental handicap cannot and will not live as happy and enjoyable a life as anyone else in society.

*What Causes Mental Handicap?*

Mental handicap can be caused by a wide range of medical, social and environmental factors, of which some are to an extent preventable. Some of the causes are still unknown, although with advanced medical knowledge much more is known about mental handicap today than even a decade ago.

It is not a recent development; there have been mentally handicapped people for as long as there have been people, and efforts to cope with their presence have been proceeding since the last century. However, as educational standards have improved, there has been a greater awareness of mental handicap in children, and improved medical skills have led to more research into its causes.

People who are only mildly mentally handicapped may have been born with average mental abilities, in the sense that there was no identifiable problem inherent in the pregnancy or birth. The mental processes may however be slow to develop if the child's early environment is not sufficiently stimulating. Many cases of mild mental handicap are thus caused by social deprivation.

In the more severe cases of mental handicap, there are various specific causes, such as the infection of the foetus in the womb, a disease in the parent, or a disease or infection in the first few days of life. Mental handicap can also be caused by drug substances taken by the mother during the period of pregnancy, or by complex metabolic disorders within the foetus itself. Accidents, either at birth or at any later stage in life, can cause mental handicap.

Other forms of mental handicap may be attributed to genetic factors, where the fusion of the parents' genes creates an irregularity in the chromosomal mix. The most common example of this is Down's Syndrome. But there are still many types of handicap—such as autism—about which little is known.

### *Can Mental Handicap Be Prevented?*

Many forms of mental handicap are caused by social factors, infection and disease, accidents during birth, drug abuse, unsatisfactory ante-natal or post-natal care or accidents in life. In all such cases, it is clear that the numbers of mentally handicapped cases could be reduced if efforts were made to counter these factors, just as increased road safety should reduce road deaths. This type of primary prevention is clearly welcomed by all involved with mentally handicapped people and the public at large.

Mental handicap can also be reduced in cases where the likelihood of having a mentally handicapped child has been shown to be higher. People who are 'at risk' of having mentally handicapped children can be advised of this, and it is safe to assume that some may be deterred from proceeding to have a child.

The incidence of mental handicap can also be prevented by its early detection in the womb through medical tests. Although such tests are not universally standard, and will only be capable of identifying certain types of mental handicap, they do introduce the possibility of the mother having an abortion to dispose of the mentally handicapped foetus. This type of secondary prevention does however raise serious and controversial issues about social and medical ethics.

*How is Mental Handicap Defined?*

The current basis for determining whether or not a person is mentally handicapped is the IQ test. Most parents now take their children to doctors at around eighteen months to see whether there is a problem in responding to basic reaction tests. The tests will also provide some early indication of physical defects such as sense impairment. It is quite possible that the parents themselves will have already noted any slow reactions if they are attentive to their child's development.

If there is any cause for concern, more controlled tests will be implemented. It may already have been established that the child is likely to be mentally handicapped; it may, for example, be known to be brain damaged, or Down's. In this case, the tests will commence early and ensue automatically.

Intelligent quotient (IQ) ratings are calculated by dividing a child's mental age by his or her chronological age. The average rating is thus 100 because a child of ten years old with a mental age of ten will score 100:—

$$\frac{\text{Mental Age : 10}}{\text{Actual Age : 10}} \times 100 = 100$$

If however the mental age of a ten-year old is only five, the IQ rating will only be 50:—

$$\frac{\text{Mental Age : 5}}{\text{Actual Age : 10}} \times 100 = 50$$

The IQ rating provides some early indication of the presence of mental handicap in a child, although it is by no means entirely satisfactory. Ideally, much more broad-ranging methods would be implemented to test a child's abilities over a range of social skills.

However, the IQ test provides some early indication of mental handicap and alerts the parties concerned to the additional efforts needed to ensure that the child's potential is adequately explored.

The threshold at which mental handicap is considered to commence is at an IQ of 70, although people with IQs of between 50 and 70 are considered only mildly mentally handicapped, and most children in this category will pass through the educational process along with other children. This group covers around 80-85% of all mentally handicapped people in the country.

Where the IQ rating falls below 50, the classification used is 'severely' mentally handicapped, and there are further breakdowns in use in the medical field describing categories down to the 'profoundly' mentally handicapped with IQ ratings of under 20. This would mean that a ten-year old child in this category would have the mental abilities of a two-year old.

In educational fields, the most widely used term is educationally sub-normal (ESN) which is further split, again on an IQ basis, into ESN(Mild) and ESN(Severe).

Many terms used in medical classifications are now no longer in general use because they are now considered offensive. There is a curious tendency for such words to enter into common parlance as insults. Such terms as 'idiot' and 'imbecile' have even attained a certain respectability, to be joined no doubt in time, by such terms as 'moron' and 'cretin'. Perhaps less curious when one remembers that mentally handicapped people have always been ostracised by those who believe they live in a comfortable world of normality.

It serves to illustrate that the words used to describe the mentally handicapped are important, not least among the handicapped themselves. Children who are described as mildly mentally handicapped are often upset to hear themselves described as such, and such terms as 'children with learning difficulties' are now in vogue.

*How Many Mentally Handicapped People Are There?*

The numbers of mentally handicapped people in the United Kingdom are not recorded on any register. Calculations of the total numbers are thus very approximate, and mainly based on what are termed 'prevalence' rates. These in turn are based on sample surveys taken in various parts of the country.

The most frequently quoted prevalence rate for all types of mental handicap is around 20 per 1000, ie for every 1000 people in the country, there are twenty people who are mentally handicapped. As there are 56 million people in the country, we can arrive at the following calculation:

$$20 \text{ per } 1000 = 20 \times 56 = 1,120,000$$

Prevalance rates for severe mental handicap are, however, considerably lower than this, perhaps four per 1000, and given the more limited life expectancy in more severe cases, the most frequently quoted rate for severe mental handicap is 3.2 per 1000 suggesting that there are around 160,000 severely mentally handicapped people in the country.

Such estimates are of course open to re-assessment and potentially subject to considerable regional contrasts.

### *What Are the Chances of Having a Mentally Handicapped Child?*

Around 6-700,000 babies are born in the United Kingdom every year. Of these, around 3,000, or 0.5% are born with some form of severe mental handicap. The chances of having a severely mentally handicapped child are one in 200.

At the point of conception, the chances are undoubtedly much higher, as many mentally handicapped babies are miscarried or stillborn. 2,500-3000 abortions are conducted each year due to foetal abnormalities. In the case of Down's Syndrome, where the birth incidence is one in every 700 births (around 0.8 per 1000), 70-80% are miscarried so the incidence at conception may be one in 200 or higher.

The chances of having a mentally handicapped child may be considerably heightened, however, under certain circumstances; for example, older women are much more likely to have Down's Syndrome babies. Where the mother is over 45, the incidence rate is one in 60.

It is possible to reduce the possibility of having a mentally handicapped child to an absolute minimum; by checking out any possible chromosomal problems in early tests, taking great care during the period of pregnancy to ensure that no actions will affect the foetus, ensuring high standards of medical care, and conceiving the child at the most appropriate age. It is however impossible to eradicate the possibility of having a mentally handicapped child, and unlikely that parents will be either prepared or able to create such a perfect policy of prevention.

As a result, many women conceive at the time most convenient to their lives and seek satisfactory rather than ideal medical facilities. They will heed advice about how they should cope with the pregnancy but will probably not sacrifice almost a year of their lives to the absolute good of their coming child. But if they are concerned about the prospects of having a mentally handicapped child, they may seek tests during the period of pregnancy to discover whether their child might be handicapped. It is essential that such decisions be discussed in an environment of understanding and good sense, rather than in a climate of ignorance and fear.

## CHAPTER TWO

# THE CAUSES OF MENTAL HANDICAP

Establishing the causes of mental handicap has always proved difficult, and even today, two-thirds of cases are due to unknown factors. This covers all types of mental handicap, including mild cases where social and environmental factors are known to be important but the exact nature of the problem is less well known. Many cases of severe mental handicap are due to medical conditions and the causes are better understood, but there are still difficult areas of definition.

The following breakdown includes some of the main causes of mental handicap but is by no means a comprehensive listing.

---

**SOME MAJOR CAUSES OF MENTAL HANDICAP**

| | |
|---|---|
| FOETUS | Chromosomal Abnormalities<br>Disorders of the Central Nervous System<br>Metabolic Disorders<br>Disease and Infection |
| MOTHER | Disease and Infection<br>Drug Abuse |
| MOTHER/FOETUS | Rhesus Incompatibility |
| BIRTH | Low Weight<br>Childbirth Problems |
| NEW-BORN CHILD | Infection |
| CHILD—ADULT | Accident<br>Social and Environmental Factors |

---

## Foetus : Chromosomal Abnormalities

Mental handicap can be caused by the presence in the foetus of an abnormal chromosomal make-up. The foetus which develops in the womb originates from the fusion of two sex cells, the ovum and sperm, and comprises a series of cell structures with a central nucleus containing the hereditary material, known as chromosomes. Abnormalities, both mental and physical, may originate from the presence of additional chromosomes, or because the chromosomes of either or both parents are incompatible. Although these disorders are genetic in origin, they are rarely inherited.

The most common form of chromosomal abnormality is Down's Syndrome, which affects about one child in eight hundred live births. This is caused by the presence of an additional chromosome; normal human cells contain forty-six chromosomes, and Down's babies have forty-seven from the moment of conception.

The other main chromosomal abnormalities are:

— Cat-cry Syndrome, which causes severe mental handicap, but is comparatively rare.

— Sex-linked Abnormalities, which affect the sex chromosomes, and give rise to various abnormalities, of which some cause mental handicap.

## Foetus : Other abnormalities

Other types of mental handicap may be caused by genetic disorders, although not specifically related to chromosomes. They occur because of the presence of harmful genes, which may be impossible to detect, but are again rarely inherited. Other foetal abnormalities may not be genetic in origin, but stem from infections and diseases; in some cases, the causes may still be unknown. Such foetal abnormalities can give rise to a wide range of handicaps, both mild and severe, physical and mental.

The most common group caused by these abnormalities are disorders of the central nervous system, which give rise to anencephalus, hydrocephalus, and spina bifida; these affect one child in five hundred, and may be almost immediately fatal or treated to avoid severe mental handicap.

**Foetus : Metabolic disorders**

A range of disorders in the foetus may be caused by the absence of the correct enzymes which break down the food which the foetus absorbs in the womb. The incorrect enzyme presence can be caused by the presence of recessive genes; or simply by the absence of certain enzymes. The most common are phenylketonuria, which is a deficiency of the enzyme which converts amino-acids, and disorders caused by the inability of enzymes to cope with carbohydrates. The condition known as cretinism is caused by defects of the thyroid gland, also caused by the absence of the correct enzymes.

**Foetus : Disease and infection**

The foetus may become handicapped not because it is genetically abnormal or have a metabolic defect, but because it contracts a disease or infection while in the womb. This may give rise to some of the conditions described above. The mental handicap may also be related to brain disease.

**Mother : Disease and infection**

In most cases, the foetus will be affected because the mother suffers from a disease during the period of pregnancy, or because the womb is infected. This may result in mental handicap. Diseases which can cause mental handicap include German measles (rubella), chicken pox, vaginal disease and cytomegalovirus (CMV).

**Mother : Drug abuse**

All types of drugs may cause mental handicap if taken during pregnancy, including alcohol, nicotine, ethical drugs and over-the-counter pharmaceuticals. The degree of risk relates to some extent to the level of intake; the drugs may affect the foetus directly, or create conditions in which complications are more likely to develop, for example by lowering the birth weight, or affecting the enzymes.

**Mother/Foetus : Rhesus incompatibility**

Around 85% of people carry the Rhesus factor in their red cells, and are Rh Positive. The remainder do not, and are therefore Rh negative. If the mother and foetus are incompatible, it can cause metabolic disorders resulting in mental handicap, although the problem is solvable, and cases now rare.

**Birth : Low weight/prematurity**

Around 7% of babies born in the United Kingdom weigh less than 2,500 grams, and 1% less than 1,500 grams. There is a strong connection between low-weight births and the incidence of mental handicap, with half of the babies weighing less than 1,500 grams having some form of damage due to factors such as oxygen starvation or low blood sugar.

The low birthweight may be caused by external factors, such as smoking during pregnancy; premature babies, which may result from insufficient standards of antenatal care, will be highly prone to early infection.

**Birth : Childbirth problems**

Complications at the time of birth may cause mental handicap in the young child which might have been a normal foetus. The complication occurs during the actual process of birth, caused by difficulties in labour, or 'anoxia', known as oxygen starvation. A delay in breathing after birth can damage the brain cells, causing cerebral palsy (spasticity) and brain damage.

Anoxia may occur because the mother is over-anaesthetised, or because the umbilical cord is wrapped round the windpipe.

**Newly-born Child : Infections**

An infection in a baby in the first few weeks of life can cause mental handicap, especially if the baby is premature. The most common infections are meningitis and gastro-enteritis.

### Child—Adult : Accidents

Apart from accidental injury at birth, accidents can occur at any time in life which may cause mental handicap. Anoxia can occur during any operation involving anaesthetics causing brain damage, and the brain can be affected by permanent injury after, say, a serious car accident.

### Child—Adult : Social & environmental factors

Most of the causes outlined above refer to the incidence of severe mental handicap, and are related to medical problems. However, around two-thirds of all cases of mental handicap—including mild cases—are not caused by abnormalities or medical problems as such. The causes are complex social and environmental factors which are essentially related to the environment of the child's upbringing. The causes have been described as material deprivation, large family units, insufficient educational standards, weak family structures. There is a belief that mild mental handicap may in a sense be inherited in a way that most severe mental handicaps are not, although public understanding would be to the contrary.

This has been a brief and generalised account of some of the main causes of mental handicap, which has deliberately stayed clear of describing the types of handicaps in obscure medical terms or dwelling on the complex nature of their origin.

Perhaps two key factors emerge. Firstly, the causes of mental handicap are clearly extremely—perhaps unceasingly—varied, covering genetic problems, diseases and infections, pure accidents, abuses of the body, inherent metabolic disorders, and many unknown causes. These causes are far from clear-cut.

Secondly, the prevention of mental handicap is obviously not completely attainable, given that it would be difficult to eradicate such a wide range of causes, but the reduction of the incidence of mental handicap clearly is a sound proposition.

But the fundamental principle of prevention must be to replace affected babies with babies that are unaffected, not dead.

## CHAPTER THREE

# THE MAIN TYPES OF HANDICAP

### I Down's Syndrome

The form of mental handicap known as 'Down's Syndrome' is undoubtedly the best known type of handicap in Britain today. It accounts for around one-third of all cases of severe mental handicap in children, and occurs among all races and in all countries.

The handicap is caused by a chromosomal abnormality which basically means that there is an additional chromosome in the cells. It is rarely inherited, and there are rarely two cases in the same family. In around 60% of cases, the cause of the handicap may be related to the age of the mother, as the rate of incidence increases considerably where the mother is older. It increases from more than one in every 2,000 births where the mother is aged 20 years or less to one in 60 where the mother is over 45 years old. The age of the father is much less important, but the incidence may increase where the father is over 60 years old.

**INCIDENCE OF DOWN'S SYNDROME BY AGE OF MOTHER**

Age of mother:

| | |
|---|---|
| 20 years or less | 1 in 2,000 |
| 21-30 years | 1 in 1,500 |
| 30-35 years | 1 in 750 |
| 35-40 years | 1 in 600 |
| 40-45 years | 1 in 300 |
| Over 45 years | 1 in 60 |

Source: Lowenstein

The overall rate of incidence is one in every 800 live births, which means that around seven to eight hundred Down's babies are born every year. The rate of conception is, however, considerably higher than this, possibly 1 in 200 conceptions.

Many Down's babies are miscarried, stillborn or live only a few days. In some cases, the handicap may be so severe that the fullest possible efforts may not be taken to prolong the life of the afflicted child, and this has given rise to much public concern about medical ethics.

Although the range of handicap, both mental and physical, is considerable, the Down's population has a common physical appearance which sets them apart from other people. The physical characteristics, which include slanted eyes, a short flat nose, a short neck, a fissured tongue and stubby hands, have made them instantly recognisable to the general public, where they are more commonly described as 'mongols'. Although this is linked to their supposedly oriental appearance, the term evokes a sense of fear and loathing which conveys a grossly false impression of some of the most affectionate and kind people present in our society.

The Down's child will almost certainly be mentally handicapped, with most falling into the IQ bracket of between 20 and 40. Most of the remainder are in the 40-70 range, with the highest grades reaching almost average mental ability. In higher grade cases, some Down's people have undergone operations, either at their own or their parents' instigation, to alter the physical characteristics which have become a stigma for them.

Most Down's people have related physical handicaps in addition to their mental disability. They will have a greater than average susceptibility to infection and disease, including kidney and heart problems, lung disorders, and even leukemia. They will have lower than average life expectancy, although with improved standards of medical care, many now live into their fifties and sixties.

Because of the fissure of the tongue, the speech of a Down's person may be impaired, and many are short-sighted. They can be sluggish in movement, especially as they grow older, and may tend to be stubborn and inflexible as children.

Like other mentally handicapped children, Down's children can achieve considerable educational improvement through a consistent programme of education and care. There is a need for immediate counselling with the parents or guardians so that the child receives the correct responses from a very early age, followed by pre-school stimulus.

In earlier years, it was common for children with Down's Syndrome to be shut away by their families, and sheltered from public reaction. In most cases, this reaction was one of either pity or fear, and this still persists today, although parents are now more aware of the educational possibilities for their children and the need for early contact with other children.

The tendency of Down's children towards stubbornness and inflexibility needs to be countered from an early age. It requires a firmer discipline than would normally be the case, and this should be consistently maintained by all parties whilst allowing the child to enjoy a happy and satisfying childhood.

Although the development of social skills may be somewhat impaired by the degree of mental handicap, this does not generally represent a major problem. It is important that the Down's child attains social acceptability in terms of standards of personal hygiene and care, and toilet training, dressing, and general behaviour and habits do not usually present great difficulties; they may simply take a little longer than normal.

The Down's child will respond well to family and friends and enjoy the same feelings of affection and belonging as any other child. They are by nature very affectionate children, capable of great love touched with a sense of real innocence. Their stubbornness may lead to a heightened sense of mischievousness and humour untainted by cruelty or spite.

It is now possible for Down's children to find places in special schools from a relatively early age, in some cases from the age of three onwards. These will tend to be ESN(S) schools, but if the early period of schooling is successful in developing the child, they may move on to ESN(M) schools and eventually to normal primary schools. The barrier to this is not so much their intellectual capability, but the social stigma of their handicap, which may affect the attitudes of teachers and the parents of other children.

But the incidence of Down's is such that a process of integration would only involve one child with Down's entering one in every 20 classes in normal primary schools. This would not place great pressure on the educational system but would have a considerable impact on the educational possibilities for the Down's child and their public acceptability.

Ideally, Down's children would join nurseries and day centres from an early age, and thus have regular contact with other children throughout their schooling. In speech development, for example, it is important that they are in the company of children with normal speech when their speech patterns develop—generally around the age of five.

This process of educational integration should be sought for all Down's children save those with severe mental handicap. Their presence in normal schools would be disruptive to the general process of education and an unsuitable environment for the children concerned. The need for special schools would continue.

After leaving school, many Down's adults would be able to live reasonably independent lives if the appropriate environment were created. At present, many continue to live at home, attending adult training centres, or employed in manual work. Many are unemployed and receive no work stimulation.

Being the most widespread and physically apparent form of severe mental handicap, Down's Syndrome is relatively well known in Britain, but considerable misunderstandings persist about the nature of the handicap. It is widely believed that as Down's Syndrome is a specifically identifiable handicap with which babies are born, the possible change in their intellectual abilities will be either small or non-existent. In fact, the improvement in their educational abilities is as great as with children of average intelligence, and they react as much, if not more, to the same forms of educational training.

Would-be parents are also concerned that their Down's child would be unable to live alone and thus be isolated and lonely when they are dead. In fact, were the correct conditions created, most Down's children would be able to live more or less independent lives when they leave school—whether their parents were alive or dead.

There are of course problems in bringing up a Down's child which are not present, at least to the same degree, in bringing up a child without Down's Syndrome. And for as long as the public continue to be wary of, or feel sorry for Down's children, there will be a considerable social stigma to contend with. It is therefore unsurprising to note that parents fear the prospect of having a child with Down's Syndrome, and seek to determine, at a prenatal stage, whether their child is suffering from this handicap. The forms of screening available are discussed later in the book.

### II Autism

Despite much research, little is still known about the causes of autism, but with an incidence rate of four to five per 10,000 of the population, it ranks as a major form of mental handicap. There are more autistic children in Britain than blind children.

The causes of autism are unknown. It is believed to be probably caused by an organic abnormality of the brain dating from before or even after birth; it can occur up to three or even five years of age. There are no traceable physical defects, although around a third of cases have associated handicaps such as epilepsy or spasticity. A fifth of autistic children have a normal IQ level; a further 25% are ESN(M) and the remainder, ESN(S).

It is customary to refer to autistic children rather than autistic people because the first account of the syndrome was only written in the 1940s by Dr Leo Kanner who said:

> "The common denominator in all these children is a disability to relate themselves in the ordinary way to people and situations from the beginning of life".

He coined the word 'autism' which means 'inability to relate to self'.

Autistic children are difficult to understand due to their complete individuality; unlike Down's people, they do not have any common physical characteristics which place them apart from other people; they are often very attractive looking children. Their behaviour patterns can also be extremely individual, so that two autistic children with exactly the same characteristics may react differently to exactly the same situation. Many characteristics are akin to deaf children.

There is 'classic' autism, and forms of mental handicap where the children are said to possess autistic tendencies. The basic impairments are:

— problems in the development of language and communication, including poor comprehension; inability to express speech or no speech; inability to understand non-verbal gestures, and a tendency to repeat or 'echo' the remarks of others, often long after they have been made.

— abnormal reactions to the senses, such as loud sounds or visual images. Often, these reactions are contrary; for example, they can be very sensitive or indifferent to touch.

— abnormal bodily movements such as jumping, arm-flapping, facial grimaces, odd postures and rocking.

— difficulties in the learning of simple actions, such as learning to brush their teeth or tie their shoes because of a difficulty in imitating. Autistic children have to be taught such basic skills from behind, using their own hands.

— further abnormalities in physical reactions and development, such as erratic sleep patterns, lack of dizziness after spinning; opposite effects to drugs.

In summary, autistic children have difficulty in understanding the world as we know it. They rarely use the word 'I', generally calling themselves by their own names, and they have difficulty in seeing themselves or other people as people, rather than objects.

Autism is also unusual in that the children will often possess special skills which can falsely suggest that they are considerably more intelligent than they in fact are. These would include their physical agility with regard to fine control; visual skills in, say, doing jigsaws; a memory for exact detail without real comprehension, or an immediate recognition of music, and an ability to instantly reproduce it.

The autistic child may have any of these abilities to a considerably greater degree than a child of higher or even very high intelligence.

By the nature of the handicap, the autistic child may have severe behavioural problems. These will include a lack of normal social contact and response; a resistance to change; an attachment to objects; a lack of imaginative play; an inappropriate emotional reaction to events, and frequent tantrums especially when young. They may also be 'hyperactive', ie extremely energetic and restlessly active.

The complex nature of the autistic handicap and the individual behaviour of the autistic child has made the education of the autistic a difficult task. The process of teaching must be flexible because between the extremes of the normal and the severely autistic child are an infinite variety of degrees of severity and persistence. Education is very much based on trial and error though schools which specialise in the education of the autistic child have developed common aims.

Like other types of mental handicap, it is appreciated that the education of the autistic child should commence as soon as the handicap is identified. Most cases of autism are now identified by the age of three, and education should commence immediately based on close co-operation between parents and the relevant authorities. The schools concerned will ideally seek to educate from an early age with a view to integrating the child into the normal educational system at the earliest opportunity. It is also felt, however, that many autistic children would not benefit from this process of integration and special schools will continue to play a major role.

A great deal can be accomplished given the correct educational programme. Even autistic children with comparatively moderate intellectual abilities can learn to live useful and independent lives. At present, however, there are often neither the places nor funds available for very young autistic children to receive the schooling they need, and although they can be placed in general ESN(S) schools, they may be unable to provide the particular forms of training which the autistic child will need.

The education of the autistic child will require the same heightened degree of patience and discipline required for the child with Down's Syndrome. Great emphasis is placed on social skills, in the teaching of correct eating habits, dressing, and personal hygiene and care, as well as academic training. The ability to learn such social skills may come slowly, but can in most cases be taught so that the child learns to behave in a socially acceptable fashion even though they may have limited academic ability.

The parents or guardians of an autistic child will encounter rather different difficulties in bringing up their child than those with a Down's child, although there are some common themes which, it could be argued, operate for all children. Although their child will not be characterised by a recognisable physical appearance, the child will still often behave in what might be termed an abnormal fashion. Also, whereas the Down's child will usually be affectionate and appreciative of its family and friends, the autistic child may have difficulty in relating to his or her relations and therefore not offer the usual rewards in terms of affection and belonging. This again differs widely depending on the degree of the handicap, and autistics may be found at the farthest extremes of social and academic capability. There are young autistic adults living independent lives and usefully employed, and others who have made little or no contact with the world they have entered.

Research continues into the causes of autism and the best methods of education and care. As there is no identifiable physical handicap present, and its causes remain obscure, there is at present no method of preventing the birth of an autistic child.

## III Brain Damage and Cerebral Palsy

Babies who are born normal, but encounter some form of birth trauma or injury are brain damaged, and the nature of their handicap will depend on the part of the brain affected. In some cases, the result will be a severe reduction in the level of mental ability, but in some cases, the damage to the brain will cause mental and physical handicap, known as cerebral palsy.

The child who is mentally, but not physically, handicapped may be slow to learn academically, and be a difficult child to handle. They may be aggressive, self-abusive, and slow to move or respond to outside stimuli. Most will be educated in special schools for the severely handicapped where their academic achievements will be limited but capable of development. Firmness will again be a strong feature in their social development.

The handicap known as cerebral palsy affects around one in every 500 births. There are several forms of cerebral palsy, including athetosis, ataxia and the best known, spasticity. Spasticity, which comes from the word 'spasm', has become known as the common term for the whole range of cerebral palsy handicaps but the three forms are significantly different.

Spastic children find that when they try to move, certain muscles contract when they should expand. 'Athetoid' children find that their movements are hindered by unintentional and uncontrollable movements, and 'ataxic' children find that they cannot generally control their muscles well. In all cases, the brain has been damaged and has thus lost its ability to control motor movement in the usual fashion. One or all four limbs of the body may be affected depending on the nature of the brain damage.

Once the cerebral palsy has occurred, it will not deteriorate, and the child must be taught to learn to cope with the handicap. The spastic child may not be mentally handicapped, but cerebral palsy is the most common form of physical handicap amongst mentally handicapped people.

The mentally handicapped spastic will require all the additional educational efforts needed for more able-bodied mentally handicapped people, plus additional help to cope with their physical handicap. Because of the difficulties in communication, there has been a tendency for the intellectual abilities of people suffering from cerebral palsy to be underestimated, but this is now generally not the case. However, the presence of the physical handicap will make it more difficult for the person to eventually lead an independent life.

## IV Hydrocephalus, Anencephalus & Spina Bifida

Hydrocephalus is one of three forms of congenital malformation relating to disorders of the central nervous system, the others being anencephalus and spina bifida. The group affect around one in every 500 children born with around 1,200 births in 1982; the numbers of such births are falling partly because they are identifiable in screening programmes, and the mothers are taking what they consider to be appropriate actions, and partly due to higher standards of antenatal care.

All anencephalus children are either miscarried, die stillborn, or die within a few weeks of life. These account for around a fifth of live births in this group of handicaps, but due to the limited life-expectancy, they are not present in the community.

The large majority—around 60%—of cases in this group have spina bifida or spinal gaps. This is a major cause of physical handicap, but the insertion of valves which drain off fluid to the heart have reduced the risk of brain damage. Only 10% of children born with spina bifida are brain damaged.

The remaining 20% of births in this group have hydrocephalus, more commonly known as 'water on the brain', where an excess amount of cerebrospinal fluid is present and the head expands to accommodate it. The circumference of the head may expand to 36″ compared with the average adult circumference of 22″.

Hydrocephalus can now be treated by the use of a valve similar to that used for cases of spina bifida. This can eradicate the handicap if the operation is performed early, but mental handicap and spasticity will still have occurred where the operation has been conducted too late. In some cases, no operation has been performed and the child will live with the enlarged skull.

Hydrocephalus and spina bifida may not cause mental handicap, but where they do, the handicap can be very severe, causing blindness, severe spasticity, paralysis and profound mental handicap.

Life expectancy may be limited, although many live into their teens and twenties. Where the operation has been performed but some degree of brain damage has occurred, the child will be similar to one with cerebral palsy.

## V Other Forms of Handicap

The above briefly describes some of the main forms of severe mental handicap which might be encountered. It should be remembered that these refer, on the whole, to severe mental handicap, and that around 85% of cases of mental handicap are mild and unlikely to provoke unusual anti-social behaviour.

Children with mild learning difficulties may attend ESN(M) special schools or pass through the normal educational system. Given a little additional help along the way, they will enjoy as happy and fulfilling a life as anyone else.

The remaining forms of severe handicaps extend over a wide range of mental and physical disabilities caused by an even wider range of genetic factors, infections and diseases affecting the normal reproductory process. They will in most cases lead to brain damage, or a range of specific physical abnormalities usually identified as some form of 'syndrome'. Probably the best known are rubella and phenylketonuria (PKU) which are preventable through immunisation and dietary treatment. Other forms of mental handicap such as cretinism, caused by a defect of the thyroid gland, and various other 'syndromes' which give way to physical as well as mental abnormalities are thankfully now fairly rare, and can be prevented with correct medical care.

## CHAPTER FOUR

# THE EVOLUTION OF CARE

There have been mentally handicapped people for as long as there have been people but, before the industrial revolution in the nineteenth century, public awareness was low. The drive to an industrialised Britain brought many people from the villages to the towns, and alerted the authorities to the widespread presence of mentally handicapped people who had previously been contained within farming communities and cared for by their families.

There was also an increased emphasis on productivity and better educational standards, which drew attention to the existence of people who could not look after themselves or sustain a normal education. But if this process of change raised the issue of the care of the mentally handicapped the initial response was to seek their confinement. It was feared that if they were allowed to move freely in society they would propagate and lower the educational standards of the nation as a whole.

One organisation, the Eugenics Movement, was especially concerned that the national intelligence would be impaired if mentally handicapped people remained part of society. Sterilisation and segregation seemed to be the solution. If such attitudes are now considered contemptible, it should be remembered that the policy of segregation continued for most of the twentieth century and many people still believe today that mentally handicapped people should be isolated and prevented from having children, even though the hereditary risks are low and can, in most cases, be discounted.

Early legislation on the subject of mental handicap failed to distinguish between mental handicap, mental illness, and what was considered to be moral incompetence. As a result, some drunks and mothers of illegitimate children were placed in mental institutions, and some never came out. Surveys of long-stay hospitals exposed such anomalies in the 1960s and 1970s, creating much public concern. But this was fundamentally a different issue to whether mentally handicapped people should themselves be in institutions essentially built to treat and care for people in need of constant medical aid.

The numbers of people in mentally handicapped hospitals rose sharply from around 5,000 in 1918 to 50,000 by 1940. As the policy of segregation was continued by successive governments, parents became ashamed of their mentally handicapped children, and many of the public attitudes still existing today were formulated.

The policy of segregation continued into the 1940s, and undoubtedly any efforts—by the hospital authorities for example—to introduce the different approach favoured today, were thwarted by the preoccupations of the Second World War.

The mental institutions were run like hospitals and, with the launch of the National Health Service in 1948, the care of the mentally handicapped was transferred to the new hospital authorities. Yet only a few years later, the Royal Commission of 1954-1957 recommended radical changes with a new policy of community integration. Despite this early re-appraisal only in 1971 did the responsibility for the care of the mentally handicapped move back to the local authorities, where it now remains.

Some of the key aspects of the current pattern of the care of the mentally handicapped are:—

— the use of long-stay hospitals
— residential homes
— short-stay residential care
— the system of education
— employment and adult training centres

## I Hospitals

Those of us who have had reason to spend even a short time in a hospital will appreciate how much they look forward to the day that they can return home, even though their period spent in the hospital may have been made as pleasant as possible by exemplary care. Yet hospitals are the homes of thousands of people in this country who do not require constant medical supervision but have simply no other place they can go.

The use of long-stay hospitals for the care of the mentally handicapped stems from successive policies of containment pursued since the last century, and which have persisted into the 1980s despite the widespread understanding that it is wrong for mentally handicapped people, who are not ill and do not require advanced medical treatment, to spend their entire lives within the confines of a large establishment which is primarily concerned with medical treatment and the cure of the sick.

Mentally handicapped people were first admitted to mental hospitals as a policy of segregation at a time when it was thought most prudent to contain such people in institutions rather than permit them to roam freely in society. There was also the problem that if the parents of a mentally handicapped person felt that they were unable to cope with their son or daughter, or simply died, there was nowhere else for the mentally handicapped person to go. The provision of homes small enough to provide a reasonable place of residence was, and still is, insufficient for all mentally handicapped people in mental handicap hospitals to leave them.

Even if this were the case, there would still be the social problems experienced by mentally handicapped people who may have spent most of their lives in a hospital and find it difficult to cope with a completely new environment.

The numbers of mentally handicapped people in long-stay hospitals had risen to 50-60,000 by 1948, when the National Health Service was founded. The Royal Commission of 1954-7 advocated that hospitals did not represent a satisfactory environment for mentally handicapped people, especially children, and that their use for such purposes should be phased out. The numbers have not, however, fallen significantly, and in 1977 there were still 44,100 adults aged sixteen and over in mental handicap hospitals in England, and recent decreases in these numbers have not been anywhere near as rapid as successive governments have proposed would be the case.

Yet it is known that between one third and one half of mentally handicapped people currently resident in mental handicap hospitals should not be in hospital and could be either immediately discharged or discharged after a short period of training. A survey in 1970 found that of all mentally handicapped people in hospitals:

— 78% could walk
— 70% were continent
— 58% needed no assistance to feed, wash or dress
— 68% had no behaviour difficulty
— 84% had no sight defect
— 89% had no hearing difficulty
— 58% had no speech defect.

It is also known that there are people in mental handicap hospitals who are not and have never been mentally handicapped. They were placed in mental handicap hospitals because they were suffering from a temporary mental illness, or because of 'moral incompetence' and never released. Many such people, now elderly, have lived in hospitals all their lives and exhibit institutional behaviour which would make it extremely difficult for them to be rehabilitated.

This social problem of readjustment is an important factor in the whole policy of bringing mentally handicapped people back into the community. Conditions in mental handicap hospitals have improved substantially along with the advances made in the understanding of mental handicap and in the field of education, but life in any large institution, whether it be a prison, a hospital, or the army, is radically different to life within the community as a whole. People who have lived for very many years in any institution have considerable difficulties in coping with changes, even if the proposed changes are potentially to be welcomed. This is especially true of elderly people in mental handicap hospitals who have lived in a closed world all their lives.

To cope with the gradual discharge of mentally handicapped people from hospitals, there has been an increase in the numbers of places available in residential homes. Despite this, there are still long waiting lists for urgent adult admissions to mental handicap hospitals, and as we have noted the numbers of adults in mental handicap hospitals are only falling slowly.

One reason for this is that mentally handicapped people are living longer, and this is balancing out the reduction in admissions. And many places in residential homes are being filled by a yet unmet need in the community, especially among mentally handicapped teenagers at school leaving age.

It has for some time been considered a most urgent need to extricate mentally handicapped children from long-stay hospitals and stop their admission to them, and there has, as a result, been a sharp fall in the numbers of mentally handicapped children in hospitals. This decreased in England from 7,100 in 1969 to 3,900 in 1977, and could now be down to 2,500. It can be assumed that this will eventually bottom out to include only those children whose handicap is so great that they require constant medical supervision of a highly sophisticated nature.

It could be said that this is a battle that is being won. But children grow up and as they reach twenty years of age, the rights and concerns which have provided them with an education, and their families with a range of supports, begin to fall away. Training centres are hard-pressed and insufficient in numbers and, with job prospects gloomy for all young people, the now older parents may find it hard to cope with the constant supervision of a young mentally handicapped person who may still exhibit child-like exuberance.

For as long as these conditions persist, and until a comprehensive range of services is developed to cope with the needs of parents with older mentally handicapped children and adults, there will still be a need for mental handicap hospitals, and there will still be young people being admitted to them.

Although nobody really argues about what needs to be achieved, there are disagreements about how the phasing out of mental handicap hospitals should proceed. In general, the voluntary organisations and some health authorities believe that hospitals should simply close their doors, thus forcing local authorities to provide the essential services in the community and the government to find the cash. Others, including the DHSS in their last report on the subject[1] favour a gradual period of change with a move to small home-like settings, believing that radical changes could place unfair burdens on the families of mentally handicapped people if they are simply unable to place their children, on leaving school, in any other form of residence.

There has indeed been a trend towards smaller mental handicap hospitals. In England in 1970, there were 232 hospitals with 59,000 beds, an average of 250 beds per hospital; in 1976, the number of hospitals had risen to 275 but the numbers of beds had fallen to 53,000, an average of under 200 beds per hospital. This was mainly because of an increase in the number of small hospitals, with 40% of the total in 1976 involving units of less than 50 beds. The problem is that a great many of such units are needed, far more than are being built, if the numbers of larger hospitals are to be reduced. The two-fifths of hospitals with under 50 beds housed only 3,000 people—only 6% of the total.

It is difficult to describe life in a large mentally handicapped hospital to people who have never seen one, which is most people. The images on our television screens, emerging from fly-on-the-wall documentaries and dramatised accounts have conveyed a picture of gloom and despair; of sad lives filled with harrowing moments of violence; these are places of isolation and fear staffed with a few uncaring, and usually male, nurses.

In fact when you enter a large mental hospital you do enter a special kind of world, a village with streets and sign posts, and usually, for in such places, everyone has plenty of time on their hands, no shortage of people willing to direct you to where you want to go. And inside the buildings, there are normal everyday things going on like whist drives, discos and parties; there are shops, and a pub. The staff are mainly friendly and helpful people doing a good job; the sort of people you get in ordinary hospitals.

If this is not the image that most people have about mental handicap hospitals it is because their concept of such places is founded on the attitudes toward mental handicap prevalent in society, and

1 'Care in the Community', July 1981

on various myths surrounding mental handicap which persist to this day. Because of the early efforts to contain and isolate mentally handicapped people and because of the lack of distinction between the mentally handicapped and those who may be mentally ill, possibly dangerously so, considerable fears have spread through society about people who live in asylums and 'loony bins'. (In fact, far from being considered inappropriate, the word 'bin' is now thought highly suitable among people who work with the mentally handicapped to describe large hospitals, but the irony tends to elude the general public). Within these places, it is often supposed, reside mad people who sometimes have to restrained in straight-jackets, defecate in public, and constantly take off their clothes.

In reality, one finds people reading newspapers, knitting and drinking cups of tea, but this constitutes rather dull television. Documentaries still seek the sensational and thus help to compound the fears of the public about mental handicap hospitals.

This is not to suggest that life in a large mental handicap hospital is a fulfilling experience; on the contrary, it has already been established that such places should not ideally exist and do not represent a suitable home for mentally handicapped people. Such criticisms which may be made must, however, be made with a sense of reality, and with the understanding that many hospitals have tried hard to create a favourable atmosphere, and that considerable advances have been made in the care of mentally handicapped people inside large hospitals. The arguments against housing mentally handicapped people in such institutions are not founded, in the main, on the premise that they are badly run or insensitive to the needs of their 'patients', but rather that no mentally handicapped person should be institutionalised and segregated from the community as a whole unless they require hospital and medical care. It is on this basis that efforts to remove people from mental handicap hospitals should and will continue.

## II Residential Care

If mental handicap hospitals are to be phased out, a comprehensive range of alternative facilities and services will be required for the care of the mentally handicapped. The best place for a mentally handicapped person is with their family, but this may not always be possible, particularly as the person grows older. Even if they can remain with their families, they may place demands on the families which will make it hard for them to cope. Some parents, such as one-parent families or those in difficult circumstances may have considerable need of support services.

What form should these services take, and to what extent are these needs currently being met?

If the parents of a mentally handicapped child immediately reject the child on realising that it is handicapped, or find that life with the child is so difficult that they feel unable to cope, it falls upon the state to find an alternative place of residence, in particular on local authorities. Efforts are initially made to persuade the parents to bring up the child at home, but where this does not prove successful or is not considered a wise step, some form of full-time residential care is required. Apart from the mental handicap hospitals, there are only two remaining options:

— fostering and adoption
— long term residential care in a home.

Although there is no shortage of childless couples in Britain, there is a shortage of couples prepared to adopt or foster handicapped children, and as a result the numbers of fostered and adopted children remain small. According to the government White Paper in 1971,[1] there were only around one hundred mentally handicapped children with foster parents or in private lodgings, and the numbers of fostered and adopted children with mental handicap are still believed to be very small.

There is therefore a real need for the adequate provision of residential homes catering for long stay mentally handicapped children, and an equal need that such homes offer the right type of care for the young mentally handicapped child.

The need for the adequate provision of permanent residential homes increases substantially as the mentally handicapped child grows up. At school leaving age, parents who had previously been

1 'Better Services for the Mentally Handicapped' HMSO, 1971.

able to cope with a child attending or possibly boarding at a special school are faced with the continuing prospect of full time life with their mentally handicapped son or daughter who may be unable to find a place in a training centre or enter full time education. Even if they are able to find employment or occupation, it is not felt that families should be forced to provide a home for their handicapped son or daughter until they are too old to do so, or that this is necessarily the best thing for the development of a mentally handicapped adult who could derive considerable stimulation and benefit from living apart from their family. The mentally handicapped person should, wherever possible, be encouraged to live outside his or her home with a view to eventual independence. Should this be achieved, the frequently cited fear of many parents of not being able to look after their children when they are old would cease to be a matter of concern.

This demand for residential homes has as we have seen risen because of the decrease in the numbers of mentally handicapped children and adults living in hospitals. Such homes are also essential support services for families in which the mentally handicapped child or adult remains at home, and where there is the need for short-term respite from the constant supervision of the mentally handicapped person. Such short-term care can provide the parents with children who are difficult to handle with an essential break, and affords an opportunity for older mentally handicapped people to gain more independence. As is the case with full time care, the ideal form of short-term care is fostering, but here it is again difficult to find the potential foster parents.

Before discussing what form short and long term residential care should ideally take, it is important to note that local authorities have been extremely slow to provide any kind of residential care for the mentally handicapped. Although due emphasis has rightly been given to the quality of the care, the first priority is the provision of sufficient places in residential establishments. Such places are still woefully inadequate.

In 1969, there were approximately 1,800 places for mentally handicapped children and 4,300 places for adults in residential homes in England and Wales, covering both short and long stay establishments. As the following table shows, this was well below the required numbers, as was the availability of places in foster homes and private lodgings.

**PLACES FOR MENTALLY HANDICAPPED CHILDREN AND ADULTS IN RESIDENTIAL CARE IN 1969: ENGLAND AND WALES**

| | CHILDREN | | ADULTS | |
|---|---|---|---|---|
| | Provided | Required | Provided | Required |
| Local authority & voluntary homes | 1,800 | 4,900 | 4,300 | 29,400 |
| Foster homes & lodgings | 100 | 1,000 | 550 | 7,400 |

Source : Better Services for the Mentally Handicapped, 1971

Out of 174 local authorities, 97 or over half had no residential care facilities for children and 24 had no arrangements at all. The report presenting these figures stated that 'in many parts of the country facilities for residential care outside hospital are still nil or minimal' and described the provision as representing a 'gross shortage'.

In the thirteen years since these figures were announced, the progress which has been made has been unsatisfactory. In 1982, there were around 3,200 places available for children and 15,800 for adults in places of residential care. Both fall well short of what was considered a reasonable requirement in 1971. As a result, there is a continued shortage of residential care facilities for the full-time residence of mentally handicapped people which is perpetuating the need for mental handicap hospitals to house them, even though it is recognised by all parties that this is to be avoided at all costs.

In addition, the gross shortage of short-term residential care facilities is placing great strains on the parents of mentally handicapped children who are unable to gain respite from the considerable commitment they have undertaken. If parents are to be encouraged to bring up mentally handicapped children at home, it is essential that they receive this type of short term respite on a regular basis. Although no separate figures are yet available on short-term care facilities, the consensus is that they are inadequate at the present time.

If local authorities do seek to improve their residential care facilities, what form might this take?

As previously noted, the ideal type of short or long term residential care is another family home. However many couples who have been unable to have children, are, understandably, reluctant to adopt mentally handicapped children. Nor is it likely that such thwarted parents would make ideal parents for a mentally handicapped child. Better chances of adoption lie with larger family units with a sense of community concern and involvement, but it is clear that prospects of a widespread programme of adoption are grim.

The prospects for fostering are undoubtedly better, and this is an area where local authorities have had a measure of success. There remains the problem, however that long-term foster parents—and people who adopt mentally handicapped children—will themselves seek short term respite from the commitment they have made. The need for short term care is therefore of paramount importance, yet this is a facility felt to be lacking throughout the country.

Where surrogate parents are unavailable, residential homes should be both small in size and fully integrated into the community as a whole, whether they be for short or long stay care, for children or adults. At present, many residential homes for adults run by local authorities have over 25 residents, whereas it is felt that no residential homes should have more than twenty-five places and that it would be much better if the average size was much lower. Again, it comes down to the concept of institutionalisation and the harmful effects on mentally handicapped people living with large numbers of other handicapped people as opposed to integrating freely with the community at large.

The ideal aim is therefore to have all mentally handicapped people in ordinary houses which would be as far removed as possible from the concept of a 'home' in the worst sense of the word, and as near to the idea of a home in the best sense.

One method of operation is known as the 'core and cluster' system, which has already been tried in several parts of the country. A number of group homes, which are either staffed or unstaffed depending on the age and ability of the mentally handicapped people, are serviced by one central resource centre which has no residential places. The network can be used for short or long term care and for all degrees of mental handicap. For older mentally handicapped children, it offers an excellent method by which they can develop independent domestic skills without being placed in total isolation.

Although such schemes suggest high staffing ratios, this may not be the case if mentally handicapped people are given adequate opportunities to live independently and care for themselves. The result would simply be a shift in staffing to increase the ratios where they are most needed, with for example severely mentally handicapped children.

Were residential care facilities to evolve along these lines, life would be more fulfilling for mentally handicapped people and for the people who care for them. But lack of resources remains a serious problem.

It costs about £100 a week to keep a mentally handicapped adult in care and over £200 a week to look after a mentally handicapped child. Central government is pruning local authority spending, and the cuts are being felt.

Clearly there is a long way to go, and this lack of financial resources is not helping. Local authorities have nowhere near enough residential care places of any sort, let alone the kind of places considered most appropriate to the needs of the mentally handicapped. Yet it can be seen that the provision of residential care, in particular short term care, is vital to the future of our mentally handicapped community.

## III Education

Although the term 'untrainable' may still be found in official classifications of mental handicap to describe the profoundly handicapped, it has been recognised officially since 1971 that no child is ineducable. In that year the Education Act, piloted by the then Secretary of State for Education, Margaret Thatcher, came into force, placing the responsibility for the schooling of all mentally handicapped children with the local education authorities. Special schools for mentally handicapped children now exist throughout Britain.

Prior to the 1971 Act, the education of mentally handicapped children was governed by legislation dating from 1944, which advocated a selective procedure to determine which children were considered educable and which were not. Those denied an education remained in hospitals without any form of mental stimulation or simply stayed at home; a few attended 'junior' training centres.

The idea of special education is to provide a special form of education for children who are severely mentally handicapped, as opposed to the form of education they would receive within the established system. Wherever possible, mentally handicapped children should attend normal schools, and thousands of mildly handicapped children do so. But more severely mentally handicapped children would not derive sufficient benefit from the normal schools, and their presence within them would present the teachers with a disruptively broad range of intellectual ability. Special schools are not therefore designed to isolate mentally handicapped children but to provide them with the specific form of education they require.

The numbers of special schools in operation in England rose from around 400 in 1970 to 1,050 in 1980. In addition there were another 550 schools for physically handicapped pupils which would include some mentally handicapped pupils who are also physically handicapped.

The original division between those mentally handicapped children who were considered educable and those who were not formed some basis for the future classification of the mentally handicapped. The terms used were ESN(S), or severely educationally sub-normal, and ESN(M), variously used to describe mild, moderate or medium handicaps. Recent thinking is that these should be scrapped and replaced with the wider concept of children with 'learning difficulties' having 'special educational needs'.[1] The idea is to drop the notion that the handicapped and the non-handicapped are separate groups, whilst still acknowledging that certain children, possibly a fifth of all children educated, may require some form of special education. In this respect, the work of charity schools will continue to play a vital role.

Due in part to this continued policy of integration, the numbers of children attending special schools for the mentally handicapped are now falling. The number of mildly handicapped children in special education fell from 76,000 to under 70,000 in England between 1976 and 1981. This included decreases in the numbers of day pupils in maintained ESN(M) schools and the numbers attending special classes in normal schools. The inference is that more pupils are attending ordinary classes in normal schools.

The numbers of pupils attending ESN(S) schools have also decreased, from 32,400 in 1978 to 30,500 in 1981. This includes some decrease in day pupils, who may have found places in ESN(M) schools, and in severely handicapped children attending schools within hospitals. In 1981, however, there were still 3,300 children being educated in hospitals.

In what ways does 'special education' differ from the normal educational process?

Mentally handicapped children, especially those with severe handicaps, need to be taught social skills which may be naturally acquired in a comparatively short time by children of higher intelligence. Although academic training, however limited, will be made available, special educational needs may involve the teaching of fundamental social and domestic skills in addition to the academic work. Most normal schools provide a smattering of social education but a special school will concentrate far more fully on these additional educational needs.

1 'Special Educational Needs', the Warnock Report 1978.

In many respects, however, life in a special school is like any other day or boarding school, and it would be wrong to assume that rare and special things go on in a special school. Teaching any type of child requires patience and understanding fused with the necessary degree of firmness and discipline; so it is with mentally handicapped pupils although the extent of the patience—or firmness—may be considerably broader.

A much higher proportion of special schools offer boarding facilities than ordinary schools, especially those run by voluntary organisations. Apart from the short-term respite this offers the families, it provides an opportunity for houseparents (staff looking after the children on a residential basis) to continue the comprehensive teaching of a full range of social, domestic and academic skills. Whether the children board or not, it also falls upon the parents themselves to perpetuate this educational process, and ideally there should be close contact between all parties concerned. This again is not fundamentally different to the education and upbringing of any child but the degree of involvement should be considerably greater.

It is now widely realised that a comprehensive education for a mentally handicapped child should continue over a longer time than the normal educational period of 5-16 years. Again, this is not radically different from the attitudes of many parents towards children of higher intelligence, who believe that their children should experience pre-school education, perhaps attending a play school or nursery from the age of three onwards, and then encouraging them to pursue further education at school leaving age. These additional educational requirements are considered essential rather than beneficial for mentally handicapped children.

The logic of early education is that if mentally handicapped children are given stimulation in their formative years, almost from the moment of birth, difficult behavioural problems can be avoided, and considerable academic advancements can be achieved.

One development in this respect is known as the 'Portage' programme, where the parents of the child are taught how they might best develop the potential of the child in a home environment. Special schools are also developing nursery facilities in order to work with children at a very young age. In some cases, it is felt that if play-schools and nurseries will accommodate mentally handicapped young children this will in itself provide them with an opportunity to share early experiences with other young children, and encourage the concept of immediate integration into the community.

This policy of constant education must inevitably extend to the continuation of the educational process beyond normal school-leaving age. Mentally handicapped adolescents are now able to continue their education beyond the school-leaving age to nineteen, and incorporate the essential social skills for independent living as adults wherever possible. It must be remembered that a child with an IQ of 50 may only have the mental age of nine when they leave school, although their social abilities may be reasonably comparable with their actual age.

Considerable progress has been made in the education of mentally handicapped people since the legislation in 1971. In 1983, the 1981 Education Act came into force,[1] setting up a new framework for children with 'special educational needs', whether they attend ordinary or special schools. This new line of thinking replaces the traditional ESN(M) and (S) categories and places more emphasis on the individual needs of the children. Fuller emphasis is placed on the need for early and late education.

Despite these important advancements, however, the problem of what happens to mentally handicapped people when they reach the later school-leaving age of nineteen remains, and what happens when they may face the prospects of a lifetime of unfulfilment which could quickly undermine the considerable efforts made by teachers, houseparents, parents and guardians to help the mentally handicapped child attain his or her full potential.

## IV Employment

In a statement published in 1981,[2] Professor Peter Mittler, a leading figure in the development of mental handicap services in

1 The Warnock Report.
2 'Mental Handicap in the Eighties' Mencap, 1981.

Great Britain stated that 'like all fellow citizens', mentally handicapped people have a right to:

— "work which is meaningful, satisfying and paid."

However sound this may be, it is of course the case that many fellow citizens are themselves being denied this right by an economic climate which has made millions of people unemployed, and which has struck particularly at young people seeking manual work. It has always been difficult for mentally handicapped people to find employment when they leave school, but now the prospects are grim indeed.

On leaving school, mentally handicapped people face two principal options in terms of employment:

— a place in an adult training centre
— full or part-time employment.

Adult training centres are operated by local authorities and supposedly provide a place of further training for mentally handicapped people with a view to eventually placing them in employment. In reality, the training centres are a place of occupation, usually involving work which is menial and unfulfilling, and from which there is little throughput into employment elsewhere.

Even places in the adult training centres are inadequate. The 1971 White Paper laid down the following requirements for adult training centres and showed the actual provision in 1969, as shown overleaf.

Since then, it has been established that the requirements stated in the White Paper were themselves inadequate, and that 75,000 places will eventually be required in England alone. A follow-up report published in 1980[1] however showed that in 1977, only 39,000 places were available in adult training centres, just over half of those required. It was further suggested that there were considerable regional contrasts with some local authorities close to achieving their requirements and others seriously lacking in their provision of adult training facilities.

1 'Mental Handicap: Progress, Problems, Priorities' DHSS, 1980.

**PLACES PROVIDED AND REQUIRED IN ADULT TRAINING CENTRES IN 1969 : ENGLAND AND WALES**

| | *Provided* | *Required* |
|---|---|---|
| For adults living in the community | 24,500 | 63,700 |
| For adults on day release from hospitals | 100 | 9,800 |

Source: 'Better Services for the Mentally Handicapped'

Official figures now show that adult training centres are full, partly because there are not enough centres and places, and partly because it has become increasingly difficult to place mentally handicapped people with firms on a full-time basis.

The first point to note here is that there has to be a balance of need. It is neither more nor less important that a mentally handicapped adolescent finds a place of work than it is for any other adolescent. So although one would seek to eradicate any sense of prejudice against employing mentally handicapped people, there is no justification for positive prejudice on behalf of the mentally handicapped. However a number of options are open to offer mentally handicapped people a comparable opportunity to work in the community.

Firstly, special schools should place greater emphasis on potential work skills in the last two-three years of education, and not assume that such skills will be forthcoming within a training centre or a first place of employment.

Secondly, places of further education should be available to mentally handicapped people as well as others, including youth opportunity schemes, thus widening the range of opportunities available beyond the adult training centres. Ideally some of the training centres should be phased out with a view to developing more flexible training arrangements for a wider range of young people who may or may not be mentally handicapped.

Thirdly, special schools should establish arrangements with local firms in order to provide their pupils with early opportunities to experience work situations. At present, few schools have a positive policy in this respect.

There will however still be many mentally handicapped people who will be unable to find employment because of the severity of their handicap, and there is a clear danger that these young people will remain at home or be eventually placed in hospitals and homes with only superficial stimulation. The possible solutions will depend on the severity of the handicap, but parents should be encouraged to consider ways in which their children might remain creatively active, thus continuing the process of education rather than allowing the person to retrogress. But many parents would clearly be unable to make this type of commitment and there will be mentally handicapped people, just as there are many ordinary people, who find themselves without an occupation for a long period of their lives.

# CHAPTER FIVE

# THE PREVENTION OF MENTAL HANDICAP

The saying goes: prevention is better than cure. There is no cure for mental handicap, but there is prevention, or at least the taking of considered and intelligent precautions to reduce the risk of giving birth to a mentally handicapped child, or of a child becoming mentally handicapped.

There are three main types of prevention, known as primary, secondary and tertiary. Primary prevention is before the moment of conception, when parents 'at risk' of giving birth to a mentally handicapped child can be advised of the risks. They may be at risk because of identifiable genetic disorders which are known to be present, or because of the age of the mother. Primary prevention of this type is not really preventive; it offers no answer to the parents at risk other than they do not proceed with their decision to have a child.

The second form, secondary prevention, concerns the child when it is in the womb. This can take the form of advice to parents, following tests on the foetus, about the possibilities of having a mentally handicapped child. If there is a problem during the pregnancy, such as an infection or disease, further tests are needed but the parents can be advised anyway of the risks present because certain infections are known to cause mental handicap.

Tests may be conducted during the pregnancy to establish whether certain types of mental handicap are present. This 'screening' for mental handicap is not as yet widely available except to older mothers where the incidence of Down's Syndrome, the main type of mental handicap which can be identified through these tests, is considerably greater.

If a baby is expected to be born mentally handicapped, the only method by which secondary prevention can operate is through abortion. Natural prevention is in operation to the extent that a greater than average proportion of the affected children will be miscarried or stillborn. Obviously this is not always the case, and if the parents do not wish to have the child because of the risks of mental handicap, the only course of action is termination. As the tests currently available occur well into the pregnancy period, this raises important moral and ethical issues, especially as a large proportion of parents are opposed to abortion on any grounds. Many people believe that abortion on the grounds of mental handicap is particularly unjust. This form of secondary prevention is thus a controversial issue which merits further attention.

The third form of prevention is tertiary, where the child has already been born. Tertiary prevention will help to ensure that the newly-born child is not put at risk of becoming handicapped during the early period of his or her life.

Out of these different forms of prevention, it is clear that very few are actually preventive in nature. Advice to parents about risk, whether primary or secondary, does not prevent the child from being handicapped, just from being born. Screening tests which identify the presence of mental handicap in the unborn child do not prevent mental handicap, because the handicap is already present. The only forms of prevention which actually prevent mental handicap are concerned with advising the mother of the possibly harmful effects of certain courses of action during the period of pregnancy, and ensuring high standards of antenatal and postnatal care to prevent a healthy born or unborn child from becoming mentally handicapped.

The main types of 'prevention' are described below.

## I Genetic Counselling

Genetic counselling is basically giving advice to parents, including those who have already given birth to a mentally handicapped child, of the risks of having a first or second child with mental handicap.

In the case of parents who have either no children or normal children, there is little scope at present for identifying the likelihood of having a mentally handicapped child. Most forms of severe mental handicap are not inherited even if they are genetic in origin. It is, however, possible to identify risk factors for subsequent mentally handicapped children once one has been conceived. The mentally handicapped child may not, of course, have been live born.

To consider genetic counselling in more detail, it is necessary to return to the main causes of mental handicap, and identify the extent to which genetic disorders are involved. It must be noted that over a third of causes of severe mental handicap are now known.

## THE FIVE PRINCIPAL CAUSES OF MENTAL HANDICAP

| | |
|---|---|
| Chromosomal Disorders | 30-33% |
| Single Gene Disorders | 16 % |
| Malformations and Syndromes | 9 % |
| Environmental, eg cerebral palsy, postnatal accidents & causes | 9 % |
| Unknown | 37 % |
| TOTAL | 100 % |

Source: 'Prevention of Mental Handicap', British Institute of Mental Handicap.

*Chromosomal Disorders*

It is known that around one-third of cases of severe mental handicap are caused by chromosomal disorders, which include Down's Syndrome babies. As we shall discuss later, this is detectable through a screening technique known as amniocentesis, but this is only after the child has been conceived. Before the moment of conception, the only information available on the chances of having a Down's child relates to the age of the mother. In mothers of under twenty, there is only one chance in 2,400 that the child will have Down's Syndrome; this rises to one in every 100 when the mother is over 40. Women aged over 38 years account for only 3% of mothers, but carry 23% of all Down's babies.

Although this continues to be an illuminating fact in understanding the causes of mental handicap, it offers no real basis for prevention. The counselling involved would seem to consist of telling older would-be mothers that there is an increased risk of giving birth to a Down's child. This is unlikely to deter parents wishing to start a family at a more mature age than usual.

The chances of Down's recurring in a subsequent birth is also rare in most instances. For the most common form of Down's, accounting for 94% of all cases, the recurrence rate is about one in 100, similar to the chances of a Down's birth among women aged over 38. There are, however, less frequent types of Down's, affecting around 4% of cases, where the recurrence rate is very high, around one in 10. This would certainly deter many parents from proceeding with a second child.

*Single Gene Disorders*

A further 16% of severe forms of mental handicap are attributable to single gene disorders, and again, although these are genetic in origin, they are difficult to identify before one affected child has been born. Once this has occurred, risks are known to be very high, in some cases one in four for further births.

*Malformations and Syndromes*

9% of affected births are caused by malformations and syndromes which are again largely unidentifiable until screening occurs or the child is born. Should one affected child be born, the recurrence rate can again be high; children born with a neural tube malformation (including anencephalus and spina bifida) can be detected by screening and the recurrence rate is about one in 20.

*Environmental and Unknown Causes*

Other types of severe mental handicap are either environmental, ie caused by accidents or injuries before or after birth, and due to unknown causes.

As one could expect, the risk of recurrence in handicaps caused by environmental factors is low. An example would be cerebral palsy, or spasticity, which normally follows a 'trauma' or 'insult' to the child which causes the handicap. Obviously if this is accidental, there is no more chance than the average that it will recur, although if no accident or error has occurred, there may be some likelihood of a recurrence, perhaps one in 10.

If the causes of the mental handicap are unknown, there can clearly be no method of establishing the likelihood of recurrence. It is known from case studies, however, that some of these unknown causes are genetic in origin, and can carry a high rate of recurrence.

It is clear from this brief appraisal that prevention through genetic counselling has limited value for the first born, but is an important consideration for parents who have had a mentally affected child or at least conceived one. Counselling will advise them of the risks, if any, that they may be taking by embarking on a further conception.

## II Antenatal and Postnatal Care

Many types of mental handicap can be avoided, and their incidence reduced, if correct care is taken during the pregnancy, moment of birth, and early care of the new born child. Such measures will ensure that the child is carried successfully and born in a healthy condition. It is of course idealistic to assume that all mothers will do everything they possibly can to ensure that the child-bearing period is a success; such is not human nature. There will also always be accidental occurrences during the period from conception to birth, and errors during and after birth. Preventive efforts can, however, be made to ensure that the mother is aware of the problems of certain courses of action; that high standards of care are in operation throughout the process; that the necessary steps are taken to combat the incidence of infection and disease which may affect a healthy foetus, and that nutritional standards are sufficiently high. This may also extend to corrective diets for certain unborn children who are potentially at risk.

Some of the main forms of prevention include:

- advice to pregnant mothers about abuses which will affect the child
- ensuring sufficient nutritional standards
- vaccinations against diseases which cause mental handicap
- early detection of deficiencies and remedial action
- reduction in accidental injury

*Maternal Abuse*

Certain types of mental handicap can be caused because of courses of action taken by the child-bearing mother during the period of the pregnancy. These may have a direct effect on the child, or reduce the birthweight of the child which will in turn increase the possibility of mental handicap.

It is known, for example, that there are serious risks in heavy smoking during pregnancy. The children born to heavy smokers are on average 200 grams lighter than those who do not. If the birthweight is low anyway this could be critical but children born to heavy smokers can continue to be slower than average for some years to come. Pregnant women who smoke marijuana also place their children at risk; they are five times more likely to have deformed or underweight babies than the average.

Heavy drinking during the pregnancy can also increase the incidence of mental handicap, again partly by decreasing the average birthweight. Around 1 in every 1,000 births are handicapped due to heavy drinking during pregnancy, although the handicap is usually mild rather than severe. Heavy drinking may be 2½ pints of beer, or five glasses of wine or measures of spirits per day.

Obviously there is a question of balance here, and the possibly harmful effects on the unborn child apply also to the woman concerned and her health in general. In other words, they are abuses which are very common, and can be generally reduced by better health understanding. Even so, many people are prepared to take the risks to their health, and extend these to their child.

*Nutritional Standards*

The above abuses have an effect on the quality of the nutritional intake of the unborn child, and this also extends to other nutritional aspects. Certain deficiencies, of vitamins or iodine, can be harmful, and there are serious dangers from mercurial or lead poisoning. Much research continues into these areas.

The problem of maintaining nutritional standards in general is of less concern in the United Kingdom than in developing countries, where malnutrition can result in mental handicap; this can extend beyond birth and affect the very young children.

*Vaccinations against Disease*

If a mother contracts a disease or infection during the period of pregnancy, it can have harmful consequences for the unborn child. The mother can then be advised of the increased risks of bearing an affected child, but this offers no preventive course of action. True prevention is thus to ensure that women are immunised against diseases which can cause mental handicap in the foetus long before they plan to conceive.

Rubella is the most serious maternal infection and can cause severe mental and physical damage if contracted during the first 16 weeks of pregnancy. Unless a woman has evidence of rubella immunisation or a positive blood test, she should ask her doctor to do a blood test. If she is not immune, she should have the rubella immunisation and avoid pregnancy for six months.

The main causes of mental handicap are virus diseases such as rubella and cytomegalic virus disease (CMV). Immunisation is available for some of these infections, including rubella, although not every pregnant mother is vaccinated. There is no immunisation available at present for CMV.

There are risks involved in vaccinations, and the vaccination itself may have harmful effects, especially if incorrectly given. There is therefore a balance between the risks of not being vaccinated against certain diseases known to be prime causes of mental handicap, and having vaccinations which can themselves be harmful. It is not disputed, however, that all pregnant women should be immunised against rubella which can be responsible for one in 200 cases of severe mental handicap. It is also widely sought for cytomegalic virus desease.

*Reduction in Accidental Injury*

As many types of handicap are caused by accidental injury to the newly born child, preventive efforts can be made to reduce the incidence of these accidents. Of course, this is easier said than done, but it is thought that up to 50% of births of this type could be prevented by better standards of care.

Such preventive methods can clearly have some impact on the incidence of mental handicap, but this is comparatively small compared with the possible effects of screening techniques in conjunction with abortion. As the table shows, the preventable proportions of births of babies with chromosomal disorders and malformations are much higher by prevention than by counselling. The overall change in the contribution of these causes to mental handicap could be considerable, but only if screening techniques were widely employed and acted upon.

**REDUCTION IN MENTAL HANDICAP DUE TO COUNSELLING AND SCREENING**

| | Estimated proportion preventable by (per 1000): | | Reduction in contribution to severe handicap: |
|---|---|---|---|
| | Counselling | Screening | |
| Chromosomal Disorders | 0·02 | 0·23 | 33% to 24% |
| Single Gene Disorders | 0·15 | — | 16% to 13% |
| Malformations | 0·05 | 0·45 | 9% to 5% |
| Total Reduction | | | 58% to 42% |

Source: 'Prevention of Mental Handicap', British Institute of Mental Handicap

## III Screening for Mental Handicap

It is possible for certain forms of mental handicap to be detected in the womb of the pregnant mother by various types of medical tests. The use of such tests is a controversial issue, with on the one hand, anti-abortion lobbies arguing that life begins at conception and that therefore all abortion is wrong, through to womens' groups who believe that such tests should be available to all pregnant women of all ages, so that those who do not wish to take the risk of giving birth to a mentally handicapped child may take the appropriate actions to prevent it.

The medical tests currently available for the detection of mental —and indeed physical—handicap are limited, both in their application and availability. They are not foolproof; they carry additional risks to the health of the child; and are capable of detecting only certain types of handicap, at present mainly chromosomal disorders and malformations of the central nervous system which give rise to spina bifida (now largely a physical rather than mental handicap) and hydrocephalus. Cases of mental handicap which occur during or after birth are of course undetectable during the pregnancy, and the autistic child will appear as a healthy baby in the womb. Even the fullest and most exhaustive tests would not and will never eradicate mental handicap from society.

The four tests currently available are Fetoscopy, Ultrasound Scan, Alphafetoprotein (AFP) and Amniocentesis.

*Fetoscopy*

Fetoscopy is a direct inspection with a fibre-optic instrument. It carries a high risk of inducing miscarriage, and is therefore reserved for high-risk situations such as structural limb and craniofacial defects. It would therefore never be considered for women who believe they have a normal pregnancy.

*Ultrasound Scan*

An ultrasound scan basically takes an X-Ray of the womb, and therefore does not involve any direct contact with the body. The scan will show the position of the baby in the womb, and will also identify whether there is more than one child present. It is a safe and widely administered test.

An ultrasound scan, by presenting an image of the foetus, may show up severe structural abnormalities in the unborn child, and these may indicate mental or physical handicap. It may, for example, expose the presence of anencephalus, a severe form of physical handicap where the brain is replaced with a form of matter, and life expectancy is virtually nil. It may also expose other structural defects related to mental handicap, and it has been claimed that the latest, most sophisticated equipment can pick up a wide range of foetal abnormalities if the technicians operating the machines are sufficiently trained.

*Alphafetoprotein (AFP)*

This is a routine blood test, which establishes the level of alphafetoprotein. If this is abnormally high, further tests should follow. The blood tests have to be conducted during the 16th-18th weeks of the pregnancy, and therefore depend on the mother knowing, with some accuracy, the date of her last menstrual period.

*Amniocentesis*

This is the main form of test currently being used to detect handicap in the unborn. It will be used following a routine AFP test if this has given cause for concern, and will be preceded by an ultrasound scan in order to determine the position of the baby in the womb.

Once the position of the foetus has been established, a sample of amniocentic fluid is taken from the uterus under local anaesthetic. Again, the test has to be conducted in the 16th-18th week of the pregnancy, known as the middle trimester.

The fluid sample can be used to tell the sex of the child, or can be grown in tissue culture to identify whether there is either a chromosomal abnormality, such as Down's Syndrome, or a neural tube defect such as spina bifida or hydrocephalus.

There are certain drawbacks to the use of amniocentesis testing which parents should be aware of before proceeding.

Firstly, the test involves penetration of the womb, and carries a risk of inducing miscarriage. No large-scale tests have been made to establish the rate of risk but it has been put at 1.5%, or an average of one in 60-70. This may be compared with the conception rate for Down's Syndrome, which is thought to be one in 200. On average, around 16% of all conceptions are miscarried.

Secondly, the tests may produce inconclusive results, or expose some minor defects which may not have the effect of causing mental or physical handicap, but which may affect the child. Apart from the anxiety caused by such uncertainty and the distress concerned, difficult decisions might have to be made about how to proceed.

Thirdly, the only course of action if some form of handicap is detected, is to have an abortion, as the handicap has already been shown to be present in the foetus. If the mother objects to abortion on moral or religious grounds, the tests are virtually pointless, and certainly not worth the additional risks that they raise.

Even if the mother is prepared to have an abortion on discovery of a problem with the foetus, the timing with current tests is very tight. In the case of amniocentesis, it takes two-three weeks to grow the culture from which the presence of handicap can be detected. Even if the tests begin immediately, the earliest possible time for an abortion would be 19-20 weeks, but this would leave no time for the tests and termination to be organised, or for the parents to discuss the matter at any length.

At present the latest permissible time for legal abortion is 28 weeks, but by 20 weeks, the foetus is well formed, and currently doctors and gynaecologists are moving towards the idea of cutting the legal limit for termination from 28 to 24 weeks. The 28-week limit was set in the 1967 Abortion Act, and since then many premature babies born before 28 weeks have survived. Some organisations, such as the World Health Organisaton, want it brought down to 22 weeks.

It must be remembered, however, that unless the mother is prepared to take these actions, there is little point in having the tests, tests which themselves create a one in 60-70 chance of miscarriage. The problems surrounding the termination of the mentally handicapped are not just moral, but practical and medical.

In theory it would be possible to significantly reduce the incidence of Down's Syndrome, remembering that women aged 38 years or over account for only 3% of births, but 23% of Down's births. If all women aged over 35 years were screened, possibly around a third of births could be prevented.

This would require, however, all women to have abortions who are diagnosed as having a Down's child. If the legal limit for abortions was reduced to 20 or 22 weeks, this would increase the practical problems, but these would be avoided if earlier detection was made possible. Although much research is underway to achieve this, it will be some time before these are available on a national level.

There are problems enough here purely in the difficult decisions which have to be made. In practice, of course, there may be additional obstacles in obtaining either the screening facilities or planning for the abortion. It means that vital decisions have to be made quickly at an extremely difficult time for the mother, decisions which may have to be made from an ill-informed base.

*The Availability of Screening*

A recent survey[1] found that only about 60% of district health authorities were carrying out alphafetoprotein tests on all pregnant women in their district. Of the remainder, some of the main reasons or comments given for not having this policy were;

— that they offered AFP to women if they requested it, or where there was a family history of neural tube defects
— the area was low-risk and the tests considered unreliable
— the costs involved were prohibitive.

In the case of amniocentesis tests, these are not widely available to pregnant women unless their age suggests that they are at significantly greater risk of having a Down's Syndrome child. Of the districts surveyed, 35% had a policy of carrying out amniocentesis on all women aged 35 years or more, and almost 80% where the mother was over 40 years of age. So around a fifth had no policy about amniocentesis, although in all cases, tests were available on request.

1 "It All Depends On Where You Live." The Maternity Alliance.

The age policy exists because Down's Syndrome is associated with the age of the mother, but there is no causal relationship between the age of the mother and the incidence of congenital malformations other than Down's Syndrome. The demand for amniocentesis would seem to be based largely on efforts to identify the presence of Down's, where there are a considerable number of miscarriages, and only around 700 births each year. Abortion statistics suggest that around a hundred Down's children are being aborted each year.

If there is a need for screening, it is in identifying the types of congenital malformations, such as anencephalus, which will not permit the child to live for more than a few weeks. Although anti-abortionists would maintain that it is morally wrong to dispose of a child even if it will live no longer than a week at the most, many more people doubt the right of a mother to dispose of a child with Down's Syndrome who stands a very good chance of living a lengthy life.

*New Developments in Screening*

Scientific developments continue to find ways of screening for mental handicap at an earlier point in the pregnancy. If they are successful, they will reduce some of the practical difficulties created by late abortions, and perhaps the qualms of the mother about terminating the child. But early abortions will carry even more serious ethical problems.

The new developments include very early sampling of foetal tissue to detect defective genes. The tissue samples are taken from the foetus at seven weeks old, when it is only about one inch long. The second development will permit the splitting of the cells and close chromosomal examination.

This is not science-fiction but work going on now in research centres. At present, the concern is to identify serious and crippling illnesses and diseases, but the chromosomal examinations will be able to identify the presence of Down's Syndrome and other abnormalities currently identified by amniocentesis.

The logical development would be for closer examination of early foetuses with a view to detecting minor deficiencies which many babies are born with. The fears that the work could escalate into 'genetic engineering', by which all but completely healthy babies would be terminated and parents could virtually plan the child they want are futuristic but increasingly real.

Some of the notable protagonists in the debate are John and Nuala Scarisbrook, of the 'Life' organisation, who believe that all abortion is wrong because life begins at conception. Professor Scarisbrook describes the killing of human beings because they are handicapped as 'the ultimate barbarism':

> "It shows the hypocrisy of our society that we work hard for the born handicapped . . . yet before their birth we are doing everything we can to seek them out and kill them. I can see no moral difference between seeking out mongol children in the womb to kill them and putting them into gas chambers after birth. Either they are human beings or they are not".

Nuala Scarisbrook has been especially critical of the controversial work of Robert Edwards and Patrick Steptoe on live embryos:

> "Just because they are small does not make them less precious. We were all like them once. It shows the same throw-away attitude to human life which animates abortionism and the practice of sedating new-born handicapped children to death".

Certainly if it became possible to detect problems earlier in the pregnancy it would make it easier for mothers to abort their children. It will become increasingly important that such decisions are taken with a full understanding of the implications of this procedure.

## IV Abortion of the Mentally Handicapped

The Abortion Act of 1967 permits the termination of pregnancy by a registered practitioner subject to certain conditions. There are four main justifiable reasons which are:

One: the continuation of the pregnancy would involve risk to the life of the mother

Two: the continuation of the pregnancy would involve risk to the physical and mental health of the mother

Three: the continuation of the pregnancy would involve risk of injury to the physical or mental health of existing children

Four: there is a substantial risk that if the child were born it would suffer from such physical or mental abnormalities as to be seriously handicapped.

There is clearly therefore no legal difficulty involved in aborting a mentally handicapped child, or a child who is expected to be mentally handicapped. The problems are ones of ethics, which in turn come down to public attitudes to what life would be like with a mentally handicapped child.

In 1981, there were around 150,000 legal abortions conducted in England & Wales. The reasons given were:

| | | |
|---|---|---|
| Reason One | : | 1% |
| Two | : | 86% |
| Three | : | 12% |
| Four | : | 1% |

Over 50% of women who have abortions are single, and it is clear that most of these have abortions for this reason (ie Reason Two). Out of the married women sector, who accounted for about a third of abortions in 1980, about 3% were because of Reason Four.

An analysis by the age of the mother shows that out of all abortions, the proportion having abortions because of Reason Four increases with age; 8% of women aged over 45 years, compared with 0.5% among under 19's.

Only a small proportion of abortions are very late, ie from the 23rd to 28th weeks—out of 163,000 abortions in 1982 in England and Wales, 0.5% were in the 23rd or 24th weeks, and under 0.1% (about 100) from 25 weeks onwards. Most of these would be as a result of late tests for congenital abnormalities.

There is therefore no widespread procedure of aborting the mentally handicapped, and the numbers of abortions on these grounds are comparatively small compared with the total number of abortions and total births. In many cases, the tests show gross handicaps which would carry no life expectancy whatsoever. Anencephalus, for example, has no life expectancy beyond a few weeks, and even this short life span is rare.

If you believe that abortion is wrong for any reason whatsoever then there is no justification for the termination of a pregnancy on the grounds of identified handicap. This stance is a relatively clear and straightforward one, but it is more about the concept of life than the particular issue of mental handicap.

In this more specific area of debate, the issue is whether or not the child will be so badly handicapped that it will be unable to sustain a life which society would consider to be in any sense worthwhile. But this calls into question whether the potential of mentally handicapped people is fully appreciated by the people who are making those crucial life or death decisions.

If the child is certain to live only a few days, the dilemma is tough indeed. Can we reasonably maintain that a woman must continue with a pregnancy in the full knowledge that she will give birth to a baby which will be either stillborn, or live a few days, even hours?

The problem is that it is not just life expectancy that determines whether the child has this 'right to live'; often handicaps such as Down's Syndrome which is one of the primary forms of mental handicap identified by tests, are considered such a burden both to the child and the family that the pregnancy will be terminated.

If parents choose to proceed on this basis, they should do so with the full understanding that they may be aborting a child capable of experiencing as full and satisfying a life as anyone else. The life may take a different form to that experienced by most of us, and may not be rewarding in our terms, or in the terms by which society judges these things. But it may well be a happy life, and that we may be taking away.

The issue is a big one, but it gets bigger when we consider the 'life and death' issues affecting the newly born handicapped child:

> "Handicap places great strains on parents and demands—many unmet—on society. But no human being has the right of life and death over another. Because the infant is unwanted by one or two people at one point in time does not qualify it for extermination. This is not merely 'a moral issue'—it is the moral issue of life itself"
>
> Mary Bodlovic, a Probation Officer, quoted in *Social Work Today* August, 1982

## CHAPTER SIX

# THE RIGHT TO LIVE ISSUE: LEONARD ARTHUR AND BEYOND

In August, 1981, Dr Leonard Arthur, a 55 year old consultant paediatrician of Church Broughton stood trial for attempted murder. The case created legal history and brought into question the whole attitude of the medical profession to the treatment and care of the newly born, severely handicapped. In this case, the victim was a three-day old baby, called John Pearson, who had Down's Syndrome.

The incident, which occurred in July, 1980, was brought to the attention of the Life organisation who reported the matter to the police. This 'breach' of medical confidentiality was later strongly condemned by Health Minister, Kenneth Clarke, and described as a 'disgrace' by Opposition health spokesperson, Gwyneth Dunwoody, who wanted disciplinary action against the person concerned. Dr Gerard Vaughan, a former health minister, was especially vocal in condemning the action, but others took the view that the 'informer' in the case had a duty to report an action which possibly constituted a crime against another human being;

> "The fact that he (Dr Vaughan) considers such disclosure of information unethical without the consent of the patient is surely irrelevant when the patient is a newborn baby who cannot protest for himself his desire to live. It worries me that turning a blind eye to the deliberate starvation of these patients is portrayed as contributing in some way to the high ethical standards of the nursing profession."
>
> letter in *Nursing Times,* May 1982

Whatever the ethics of the disclosure, Leonard Arthur did go on trial in August, 1981, at Leicester Crown Court. The presiding judge was Mr Justice Farquharson.

The case for the prosecution was that the doctor prescribed a course of non-treatment by the administration of the drug DF118 which suppresses the appetite and impairs breathing. There was no apparent reason to administer the drug, although the quantities involved were not above the legal limits. Evidence from the Home Office consultant pathologist, Professor Alan Usher, discovered no abnormality except pneumonia due to lung statis; 'exactly what one would expect in poisoning by a respiratory depressant drug.'

The case was a strong one, not least because Leonard Arthur had admitted that if parents rejected a mentally handicapped child (which they had) it was honest and ethical from his standpoint that the child was better off dead. He thought that preferable to the child's being in an institution or with foster parents. He thought that this was 'kinder, more humane and more in keeping with informed medical opinion.' The case hinged, however, on whether the administration of the drug caused the death, and thus to a large extent, the pathological evidence. It was on this basis that the defence were able to confound the evidence of the prosecution and gain Leonard Arthur his reprieve.

The initial examination of the corpse was conducted by Professor Usher in consultation with Professor John Emery, a colleague at Sheffield University. Professor Emery was later retained for the defence, and permitted to conduct a more sophisticated analysis of the laboratory slides which revealed heart and lung defects. This new evidence was held by the defence and only came to light during the trial. This initially resulted in the charge of murder being changed to attempted murder, with Professor Usher reluctantly forced to admit that his initial examination was inconclusive. Mr George Carman QC, in his final speech for the defence, made much of this; 'The plain fact, when you come to the evidence, is that this melancholy prosecution is now in a state of retreat and disarray.' He suggested that the jury should bring in a decision that would mean that 'in future, parents and doctors could make decisions on this awful problem without unidentified informers rushing off to the police.'

Professor Usher, writing later in the *British Medical Journal,* described this as a 'distasteful legal manoeuvre' orchestrated by the defence lawyers. Of the new evidence, he wrote;

> "These new slides (tissues from the dead baby) were made privately and never shown to me, and the defence pathologist's (John Emery) change of opinion was deliberately kept secret until I was in the witness box and giving my evidence. He was actually expressly forbidden to speak to me about the matter. I was then permitted a short time during the lunch interval to study this new material before being cross-examined on it. I had to concede that they (abnormalities at birth) were present and much was made of this by the defence counsel."

It is Alan Usher's contention that if this evidence had come to light before the trial, a third opinion could have been obtained from a specialist paediatric pathologist. This might have led to the charges being dropped, or alternatively might have considerably strengthened the case for the prosecution. 'It was this latter risk that those conducting the defence decided not to take.'

Professor Usher concludes his criticisms of the defence counsel's actions with this damning comment:

> "Whether they (the abnormalities) really played any significant part in the fate of this baby, kept without nourishment or antibiotics and given dihydrocodeine in doses slightly more than twice the average fatal level for adults, is entirely a matter of opinion."

Clearly, then, Professor Usher remains convinced that the baby had at least an 80% chance of survival, and that Leonard Arthur did prescribe the drug with the intention of causing the child's death, especially in view of Dr Arthur's comments on his philosophical attitude to this type of situation.

Behind Leonard Arthur, however, stood the vast majority of the general public, who flooded him with letters of support during the trial. The common view was that the futures of severely handicapped babies should be determined by parents and doctors, and not subject to legal intervention. The view of the British Medical Association is that as every patient has a right to refuse medical treatment, it is reasonable for parents to decide for babies. J. D. J. Harvard, the Secretary of the British Medical Association clarified the medical attitude in a letter to the *Daily Mail* in July, 1982:

> "all babies have the right to be fed and cared for, except where there is an incurable deformity and where the baby would suffer pain and distress if feeding were attempted."

This was clearly not the case with John Pearson, however, who did not have an incurable deformity, nor was unable to feed. Rather, one of his difficulties was that he was not fed.

Considerable criticism was also made of the judge's summing-up in the case, which some felt failed to clarify the real issues. Comparisons were made, for example, with mercy killing, such as suffocating a sick and elderly relative suffering from an incurable disease, which implied that the child was better off dead, and likely to die anyway. Although the subsequent pathological tests had suggested complications, there was no evidence to suggest that survival prospects were unreasonable.

The judge further delivered this remark:

> "I imagine you will think long and hard before concluding that doctors of the eminence we have heard here and others in that great profession have evolved standards that amount to committing crime."

The 'eminent doctors' had given evidence in the trial to the effect that it was acceptable to 'invoke a regime of starvation and sedation to quickly speed the demise of the handicapped child.' One has said, as Leonard Arthur himself believed, that 'in such circumstances, with parental consent, it could be right to end life.'

The repercussions of the Leonard Arthur case were enormous. For the first time, a public debate began over whether doctors, in consultation with parents, had the right to terminate life because they believed that the life concerned was not worth the living.

It is certainly true that much of the criticism of Leonard Arthur and doctors who believe as he did, was made 'in ignorance and misunderstanding of how the science and art of paediatrics is practised' as the defence counsel in the case claimed. We know that doctors have to make very difficult decisions which are sometimes about life or death. Sometimes, this may be whether to save the life of the child or the mother. But there is no real decision which has to be made about whether a child should live or die, for nobody has the right to make such a decision. The only course of action is for the doctor to make every effort possible to save the life of the child concerned, whether the parents approve or not. In the case of profoundly handicapped births, life expectancy will probably be limited anyway; if it is not, the doctors and parents are, in effect, destroying the life of the baby concerned because they are making subjective judgements about what kind of a life it will lead.

To open the door to this type of possibility is to accept that babies who are mentally handicapped, yet perfectly capable of leading a happy life with either their parents or guardians, are deprived of this opportunity by a small group of people who know little about what this life will be like.

In the case of the parents, they are unlikely to be in a position to make a rational judgement. Most people have little contact with mentally or physically handicapped people and, as we have discussed, base their attitudes and opinions on historically inaccurate concepts. They have lived all their lives with this sense of fear and in ignorance of the lives of our mentally handicapped population, yet are then confronted with a mentally handicapped baby. The fear and revulsion felt by such parents has been well documented by the many parents who have initially wanted their child to die, and then gone on to bring up and care for their mentally handicapped child.

Many parents suffer considerable shock on the news that they have a mentally handicapped child, and many who go on to keep and raise the child freely admit that their initial reaction is to let the child die. A representative attitude may be found in a letter to the *Daily Mail* in April, 1982, here abridged:

> "I am the mother of a spastic child but had I been told before his birth that my son would be handicapped I would have asked for an abortion. Had I been told at his birth that he was not 'normal' I would probably have hoped he would have died before being taken home from hospital. Four years with a handicapped child have taught me a lot of things, but three in particular:
>
> "First, had I chosen to have an abortion or for him to be allowed to die, I would have made the biggest mistake of my life.
>
> "Second, however severely handicapped your child is, there are parents looking after children less fortunate than your own and managing incredibly well.

> "Third, and most important, there are parents who are not able to cope with a handicapped child themselves.
>
> "Please let us never condemn the handicapped child or the parents to whom the strength is not given."

The view taken here is that parents may not be able to cope, and certainly they will feel this when they first discover that their child is handicapped. In time, however, they may learn to cope and discover a great deal in the child they have raised, which may lead a life which is no less happy, but just 'different' to that of others in some ways. If they do find they cannot cope, services are available to look after the child.

But if loving parents freely admit that they would have chosen to let the child die if given the choice, it is clear that the vast majority of parents would take this view if given an option by the doctor concerned. The onus thus falls very heavily on the doctor, who may in fact have to persuade the parents to allow the child to live; this would be the case if a life-saving operation is involved.

If the 'moral dilemma' is that facing the doctor rather than the parents, we must consider whether doctors are sufficiently aware of the considerable developments in the care and treatment of mentally handicapped people to make the correct judgements. There are many who believe they are not, including many in the profession.

One such is Dr Campbell Murdoch, a senior lecturer in general practice who made a study of Down's Syndrome in Scotland. He believes that the medical profession is encouraging Down's babies to die at birth because of ignorance and fear. He has attacked what he calls the 'practice in many of the country's paediatric units to avoid performing life saving operations unless their parents insist;

> "we pour cold water on the natural loving feelings of their parents, and give them the impression they have produced something monstrous. Parents in this situation know they have got a problem on their hands. They need the information which will motivate them to care for the child. The Leonard Arthur case was the tip of the iceberg as far as I was concerned."

Dr Murdoch resigned from the British Medical Association over its attitude to the Arthur case, but criticism has also come from within the BMA. Following the case, several doctors expressed concern at the information which came to light during the trial;

> "I believe that a newborn child has the right to be fed, warmed and cherished. This basic right cannot be abrogated by the decision of the parents, the doctor or the State. In all respects these are ordinary means of sustaining life and must not be withheld."
>
> Dr Ian Jessiman

> "No longer do we as a profession support the termination of one individual to ease the discomfort and social inconvenience of the other. Whom shall we terminate next? The elderly, the young chronic sick, the unproductive in monetary terms?"
>
> Dr Dermot Lynch

The legal profession was also concerned about the outcome of the Leonard Arthur case. Ian Kennedy, Reader in Law at King's College, London, who gave the 1980 Reith lecture on medical ethics, felt that firmer legal guidelines were required to ensure that handicapped babies were not left to die, and that the decision could not be left to parents and doctors. He criticised the judge in the Leonard Arthur case for indicating that it was lawful to treat a baby with a sedating drug and offer no further care by way of food or drugs or surgery, provided certain criteria were met.

The general outcome of the Leonard Arthur case was a call for clarification of some of the issues involved. Certainly it provoked wide media interest which continues today, and it remains a highly emotive issue.

Such was the interest provoked, that the Human Rights Society commissioned MORI to find out public attitudes to the 'right to live' issue. Of the sample:

- 45% thought that it was wrong to withdraw food and medical treatment from severely handicapped babies rejected by their parents.

- 37% thought it should be arranged for the baby to die

- 18% did not know.

Although this was welcomed as showing that a 'majority' of the public were opposed to allowing children to die, it is a sad comment on the public's understanding of mental and physical handicap that almost two-fifths thought that this was acceptable.

A subsequent survey was conducted in September, 1982 to assess attitudes within the medical profession itself. The survey was conducted by *Hospital Doctor* on 200 doctors, and asked whether the doctors felt that there should be greater curbs imposed on a doctor's right to determine the survival of a grossly handicapped newborn baby. The result was:

| | *Consultants* | *Juniors* |
|---|---|---|
| Yes | 13% | 23% |
| No | 77% | 71% |
| Don't Know | 10% | 6% |
| Total | 100% | 100% |

It is significant that most comment on the issue has referred to the 'severely' or 'grossly' handicapped babies, rather than just mentally or physically handicapped babies. This suggests that it is only a possibility where the baby is so handicapped for any reasonable human existence to be impossible. In the public debate on this issue, much has focussed on what is termed the 'disputed territory' of whether human life is present in any reasonable form.

This is, however, a dangerous concept. If we accept that in extreme cases certain babies should be allowed to die, we place doctors in a moral dilemma; there is a line to be crossed, a choice to be made. If we simply accept that no baby should be allowed to die, and every reasonable effort should be made to maintain life, then there is no moral dilemma, no difficult decision to make, and no disputed territory.

It must be remembered that children are termed 'severely' handicapped if they have an IQ below 50. Many children grow up to enjoy satisfactory lives who are clinically termed severely handicapped, yet they would apparently be at risk of being allowed to die due to the severity of their handicap. It is surely wrong to draw a line between the right of another to live or die.

On this issue, the decision of the parents should carry far less weight than it does. They are probably shocked by the news, and are not in a position to make a rational decision. Yet the rights of parents to decide the fate of their child is a strongly protected one, and one which many believe should be preserved. In 1981, however, this fundamental right was challenged for the second time in another case to make legal history.

* * *

The case occurred in August, 1981, around the same time as the Leonard Arthur trial. It involved another Down's baby, a girl called Alexandra, who required a life-saving operation to remove an intestinal obstruction.

The baby was born on July 28th, 1981, and it was immediately diagnosed that she suffered from Down's Syndrome and also from a duodenal obstruction. Her parents refused consent for an operation to remove the obstruction, although there were no grounds to suppose that if the outcome of the operation was successful, Alexandra would not go on to enjoy a life of some longevity.

In this case, the doctor involved, Dr Robert Dinwiddie, refused to consent to the parents' decision, and called in the hospital social workers. The birth was at Queen Charlotte's hospital in London, and the child was made a ward of court with Hammersmith and Fulham Council at the age of four days. They immediately signed a consent form for the operation to take place.

The following day, doctors at Great Ormond Street Hospital refused to operate because the parents had not given consent. Following further parries, the operation was successfully conducted at Hammersmith Hospital.

The parents' attitude in this case was understandable. They were by all accounts, cultured and responsible people who wished the child to die in as painless a way as possible. But they were clearly under considerable stress when making their decision, which involved refusing consent for a vital operation for a baby with no other problems than those associated with Down's Syndrome; problems which once the operation had been conducted, would not prevent the child from an average life.

Dr Alexandra Macara, chairperson of the British Medical Association's ethics committee stressed the difficulties for the parents in making rational decisions at such a time. From *The Observer* in December, 1982:

> "The basic thing one must understand about these decisions is that they are desperately disturbing and agonising for the parents. It's very common for a women to be depressed after giving birth: if on top of that the parent's hopes are dashed, and life seems desperately fraught because they have a handicapped child, it's absolute hell."

Given this stress, parents are scarcely the best people to make life or death decisions about the future of their child, a fact which the doctor involved in this case clearly realised. But the intervention of the Hammersmith and Fulham Council in this case in effect created legal history—it had never happened before.

* * *

The Hammersmith and Leonard Arthur cases began a national debate over the 'right to live' issue which continues today. Each in turn raised questions about the decision-making process by which some handicapped babies were allowed to die; one by investigating the actions and attitudes of a consultant paediatrician, and the other by challenging the attitude of the parents.

In May, 1982, a similar case also challenged parents' fundamental rights. The case occurred in Rochdale, and again featured a Down's baby, this one also physically handicapped. The child again required a life-saving operation; this time to remove a stomach blockage. The parents again refused consent for the operation, but the operation was eventually successfully conducted following the intervention of social workers and a woman judge.

The actions of Rochdale's Social Services were strongly criticised at the time. One comment came from a councillor on the Social Services Committee, Jim Haggerty:

> "My view is that our officials overstepped the mark. Circumstances such as these should be the parents' decision. They must go through life

> knowing that a child of theirs is suffering a limited existence and being cared for by someone else."

Certainly the parents' ordeal was such that they were under sedation over the incident. Yet the baby survived a successful operation and is alive today.

These three cases have to call into question the rights of parents, ignorant of the lives of the mentally handicapped in our society, and fearful and shocked by the discovery that they have a mentally handicapped child, to make decisions about the future of their handicapped children. Although every parent has the right in the fullness of time to decide whether he or she feels they can cope with their child, they cannot be placed in a position of absolute power over its life if they have an extremely misleading impression of the form that that child's life might take. Even if that child's life is not 'normal' or likely to be comparable with the lives of other people, there can be no arbitrary rule which condemns certain babies to death because they do not conform to some spurious notion of that which constitutes a satisfying or fulfilling life. We could on this basis begin to question the lives of many people which we would subjectively consider to be less fulfilling than our own.

But if parents are not the best judge, and doctors themselves may not always be fully conversant with a real understanding of the facts, who will be the ultimate arbiter? The answer is simple; there need be no judge and no moral dilemma if parents and doctors accept that they have no more right to end the life of a handicapped child than they do for any child which enters this world. If they do so, they are making decisions which they have no right to make, because it is the doctor's obligation to save life not take it, and the parents' duty to stand by their children from the day they are born or, if this is not feasible, for society itself to step in and shoulder this ultimate demand upon it.

* * *

In a survey of medical genetics published in November, 1982 in *Midwife Health Visitor & Community News*, is an account of a couple who both suffered from 'achondroplasia', a condition which causes severe short-limbed dwarfism. The couple sought information about starting a family, and were advised that there was a two in three chance of the child being similarly affected. The response of the couple was that this was encouraging news because they were successful circus clowns and hoping to have like children to keep the business in the family.

Most of us, of course, hope to have children that we can consider 'normal'; with average or above average intelligence, and no physical defects. In fear of this possibility, many women choose to have pregnancy screenings and may opt for abortion if evidence of handicap is revealed. If they have a child who is handicapped, most parents will keep the child and grow to love him and her in the fullness of time. Some feel they are unable to cope and the child is taken into care with a view to fostering. In many instances, the mother of the child will wish to keep the child, but the father is unable to come to terms with the handicap, and the family is split up. This may also happen in reverse.

The raising of a mentally handicapped child is a long and hard road, but then many would say so is bringing up any child. The additional strain may in the end be more rewarding, more life-enhancing than one would ever have felt possible. But if the problems are acute, and the parents feel they are unable to cope, foster or home arrangements can be organised. This is fundamentally better than depriving the child of a right to live.

This may, in any event, come about through nature. Many severely handicapped children do die at an early age through natural causes, but at least the parents can feel that they did everything they could for the child when it was alive. To condemn the child in the first few days of its life, and engineer its death can only be a gross misjustice.

In considering the right to live issue, there is a tendency to fight shy of the emotive word of murder. Doctors do not kill handicapped babies; they allow them to die, implying that they would naturally die if left alone. Yet all babies would die if left alone, and the act of standing by and doing nothing is tantamount to injurious action. The difference is one of semantics; the outcome the same.

In the final analysis, it is the public who must decide. In the aftermath of the Arthur trial, Dr Michael Thomas of the BMA said:

> "We must say to the public, 'you cannot leave us without moral guidance on this. You cannot turn your back on this issue, and leave us with the responsibility'."

Only, therefore, when the public come to terms with the nature of mental handicap and break down the barriers of misunderstanding which have existed for centuries, will a real sense of understanding permeate our society. When and if this occurs, decisions about mentally handicapped babies will be made with a full consideration of the issues involved.

Dr Leonard Arthur died on Christmas Day, 1983 at the age of 58. The trial proved an immense strain, and he spent the last months of his life confined to a wheelchair. He lived 58 years longer than John Pearson, who died in Derby City Hospital in July, 1980, aged three days.

## CHAPTER SEVEN

# MENTAL HANDICAP IN THE MEDIA

The way that the subject of mental handicap is treated by the media is of crucial significance in public attitudes to mentally handicapped people. Those members of the public who have not had an opportunity to experience contact with the mentally handicapped except in the most superficial way inevitably draw their opinions from the concepts portrayed in the mass media and, above all, from what they see on television.

The main problem here is that television seeks to dramatise and explore the extremities of human life. The everyday lives of ordinary people are not the basis for good television unless the characters and events are portrayed in a consistently entertaining fashion, and over a period of time; hence the great success of television soap operas. One-off dramatisations inevitably build around a central series of events which may be true to life in what they depict, but false in the way that time is telescoped; in other words, they are played out in dramatic, not real time.

The subject of mental handicap is thus largely considered as a 'problem' area within television drama. The simple story of a mentally handicapped child or adult growing up would not be considered dramatic enough for fictional representation; the drama must focus on a series of events which create a larger than life situation, which will play on the emotions of the viewers.

Such a play on emotions could of course be depicted in different ways. A play on mental handicap, such as a period in the life of a mentally handicapped person, or depicting the effects which a mentally handicapped child has on the parents, could be either an uplifting or depressing experience. In reality, it would probably be both, but in dramatic form, some emotional focus would be sought. Sadly, the dramatic depiction of mental handicap on television has been mainly concerned with the sadness and harrowing nature of the subject. And it has been in the nature of documentary television to also exploit the subject of mental handicap in a sensational fashion. Television's treatment of the subject of mental handicap remains a major barrier to real understanding among the British public, compounding the fear and ignorance which many possess.

This has not always been the case. Early in the 1970s, the BBC Horizon film 'Joey', based on the book 'Tongue Tied', a true life autobiography by Joey Deacon about his life in a mental hospital showed with sensitivity the achievements of a mentally handicapped spastic in reaching the outside world by the strength of his courage. More recently, in November 1982 BBC2 showed the Alan Bennett play 'Our Winnie', a story about a mother of a mentally handicapped teenage girl who takes her daughter to a cemetery to visit the grave of her husband. The situation was touched with sadness (the trip was ostensibly a day out for the girl, thus implying the limitations of her life's experience) and the photographs of the girl snatched by an opportunist art student for later exibition had more to do with the exploitation of human life by art than with mental handicap. But through sensitive playing and a warm humorous script by Bennett, the play went some way to portraying the normality of life with a daughter who is 'not quite right'.

Earlier in 1982, Yorkshire Television quite ambitiously built a short comedy series around the life of a 40 year old man with the mental age of ten. The series, called 'Horace', met with mixed reactions mainly because the public generally feels that mental handicap is not something one should laugh about, or at least not admit to. In practice, most people who work with mentally handicapped people both laugh at and with them, and refute the attitude that this is an exclusively sober and serious subject.

It is perhaps not merely coincidence that such recent efforts to portray mental handicap with humour and sensitivity are largely forgotten among the broad swathe of the British public. Two other recent plays, both dramatised, although one from real life, left a more lasting impression.

The first of these was shown on the opening night of the new Channel Four station on November 2nd, 1982, and regarded as the channel's first 'star' production. It thus gained a considerable audience, including many people who would not normally have watched a film of this type given the subject matter.

The film was 'Walter', adapted by David Cook from his award-winning novel of the same name. It was directed by Stephen Frears, and starred Ian McKellen as the central character, Walter.

Walter is mentally handicapped and lives in the North of England with his mother and father and a flock of pigeons—his father is a 'fancier'. Nothing goes right for Walter; his father dies early, soon followed by his mother, a rigid, religious woman, who treats the boy harshly but teaches him good conduct, to write and to hold down a job in a sweet factory where he is patronised by his superiors and ridiculed by his fellow workers.

The mother's death is portrayed in a macabre scene where Walter is unsure whether she has died, or even what death is, and allows the corpse to rot for a few days while he sits by her side. To add to the general gothic touch, the now released pigeons fly around depositing their droppings on the dead body. But worse is to come.

Next, we have Walter impounded in a large mental institution with other inmates, played by real mentally handicapped people. On his first night, he is homosexually attacked by a mentally handicapped dwarf, and there then follows a parade of evils which serve to emphasise the horrors of life in a mental hospital—attacks on patients by the staff, general squalor, lack of hygiene and overcrowding; essentially harrowing and horrific.

The original novel from which the film was adapted was light, comical and whimsical, yet despite the author's own involvement in the adaptation, the film version was unrelentingly crude and insensitive to the subject it was treating. Brian Kirman, writing in the *British Medical Journal* expressed the sentiments of many:

> "The whole effect (of the film) was destructively negative, and there was no attempt to spell out constructively ways in which services for the mentally handicapped might be improved. In the portrayal of the institution, which was dominated by a brutish regime and encrusted in excre-

> ment, there was no indication whether this was present or bygone circumstances."

In fact, the film was set in the 1950s, but it is doubtful whether any but a few of the millions who watched the film appreciated that life in a mental hospital is any different today. It is also doubtful whether many hospitals were like that then.

If the central character emerged with any sense of dignity, it was at the considerable expense of the other mentally handicapped people in the film, some of whom actually were mentally handicapped. The general theme was that Walter could muddle through with Mum and Dad, but because they died, he ended up in a horror show.

The film has undoubtedly done much to compound the fears of the public about mental handicap, and on a number of levels.

Firstly, it depicted the life of a mentally handicapped person as being unrewarding, unstimulating and confined. Walter is seen to be best in the care of his parents because they protect him and offer him a barrier against the outside world. Yet this environment would be suppressive and unfulfilling for a real 'Walter'.

Secondly, the film suggests that Walter is thrown into a harrowing situation because his parents are dead, compounding the fears of many people that if they had a mentally handicapped child, there would be no-one to look after him or her if they died.

Thirdly, it depicted a mental hospital as containing mentally handicapped adults who were sexually perverse or completely unable to look after themselves; suggesting that this was typical of most mentally handicapped people. The brutish, uncaring nature of the staff was conveyed as almost an inevitable necessity brought about by the institutionalisation of working in such a place; just as the public will accept that prison warders will overstep the line from time to time because of the people they are dealing with.

To return to Brian Kirman's comments on the film:

> "there was a danger that the public will be disgusted by the film and despair of any constructive solution."

Undoubtedly, 'Walter' was a fine film, if films are determined by their acting, direction, script. Ian McKellen's performance, too, had much to commend it. It is sad that such talent and thought should create such a nightmarish and harrowing depiction of mental handicap, which left viewers saddened and stunned by what they saw, and may have put back for years the progress towards a real understanding of mental handicap among the general public.

The second dramatisation to have a major impact in the 1980s was shown only a few days after 'Walter'. Broadcast on November 23rd, 1982, the Play for Today, 'John David' was meticulously balanced in its depiction of the true life dilemma facing the author of the play, Paula Milne, on discovering that she had given birth to a child with Down's Syndrome.

The following plot synopsis is taken from the BBC press release about the play:

> "Judith and Patrick are told two days after the eagerly-awaited birth of their first baby, that he is suffering from Down's Syndrome—he is a mongol. Their immediate and instinctive reaction is to reject the child.
>
> "This shattering blow and the effect of their subsequent decision on their lives is the subject of 'John David', Paula Milne's thought-provoking 'Play For Today' on Tuesday, November 23.
>
> "Judith leaves hospital and returns home alone. From hospital staff, social workers and relatives alike, the pressures on Judith and Patrick to accept the baby are very strong. Despite critical letters from their families and harrowing interviews with different social workers, they remain resolute. Then they hear that there has been a request to adopt the baby, John David, from Judith's mother, Cynthia. Judith is astonished, as she has had a difficult relationship with her mother, whom she feels has little maternal feeling. But their argument about the proposed adoption reveals the magnitude of Cynthia's love.
>
> "After some months in the children's home, John David dies. At the funeral Judith comes to terms with grief for the first time since the birth.
>
> "Paula Milne's powerful and controversial play is a fictional account of her own experience of having a mongol baby and deciding, with her

husband Peter, that they would not bring up the child. The play is based on her earlier novel 'John David'. Paula is also a well-known television writer, who has worked on numerous popular series, such as 'Z Cars', 'Angels', 'Coronation Street' and 'Juliet Bravo'. Earlier this year, her BBC play 'A Sudden Wrench' gained critical success.

" 'John David' stars Dearbhla Molloy as Judith, James Hazeldine as Patrick, Gwen Watford as Cynthia and Edward Hardwicke as the paediatrician. It is produced by Brenda Reid and directed by Rodney Bennett."

Paula Milne's novel, on which the play was subsequently based, was written in the wake of the controversies surrounding the Leonard Arthur case and the case of Alexandra, the Down's child granted an operation by Hammersmith Council against the wishes of her parents. Writing in *The Evening Standard* in May, 1982 when the original book was published, Paula Milne said:

"It's only recently that I've felt able to write about him, but the controversy about Down's Syndrome babies has brought it all to the surface. I know some people might think the decision I made was unpleasant and monstrous but I want to tell how I came to make the decision and the reasons behind it.

"A lot has been said about the marvellous people who do look after Down's Syndrome babies. I felt that somebody should give the other side . . . how such a tragedy brings all kinds of penalties in its wake."

The penalties came, in fact, from Paula Milne's, and the fictional mother's decision to reject the child, rather than from having the child. They took the form of both the grandmother and father doubting the decision and persuading her to change her mind; and from medical advisors and social workers seeking to persuade her to keep the child. In the play, such is the force of the opinion against her that one wonders at her resolution, which increasingly seems to go against common sense, decency, and even the fundamental duties of a parent.

Paula Milne's decision to dramatise these events in book and play form is as admirable as the decision to make 'Walter' and undoubtedly with equally noble intent. She felt she was speaking for millions of would-be mothers in rejecting a child because it was mentally handicapped; regrettably, she was.

Despite all the contrary opinions expressed in the play, the underlying message was that it is the mother's right to choose whether she wants to bring up a child who is mentally handicapped, and that other people simply do not understand how the mother feels.

Undoubtedly one of the underlying trends among public opinion about mental handicap is that parents should decide; whether to have the child, whether to keep it once it is born. 'John David' does not question the child's 'right to live' but in a real sense the ability of parents—mainly the mother—to accept the child into their home.

In this sense, the play focussed on one of the key issues concerning mental handicap; whether, if faced with life with a handicapped child, parents will be able to accept it and cope. Many parents and would-be parents watching the play would understand the mother's position because it reflected the consensus of public opinion. The harsh treatment of this attitude, as experienced by the mother in the play could be interpreted two ways: either as evidence of the pressure brought to bear on the parent by outside forces, even family; or as a positive sign that the mother's position was wrong fundamentally.

Undoubtedly 'John David' succeeded where 'Walter' failed in considering an aspect of mental handicap in a balanced fashion. Regrettably, most other television programmes, notably 'fly on the wall' documentaries from Yorkshire Television and Central have sought to expose the inadequate conditions in which many mentally handicapped people live, especially in long stay hospitals, rather than discuss the progressive steps being made in the care of the mentally handicapped in Britain today. Regrettably, such documentaries convey to the public an image of the mentally handicapped which is historically stereotyped—that mentally handicapped people are sad figures of rejection incarcerated in mental asylums; the images of 'Walter'. There have in fact been achievements in the care of the mentally handicapped in our society, and one of the fundamental barriers still to be broken—that of public opinion—will only come from a more positive attitude among the media to the good things that are happening. Only then will the public begin to realise that mental handicap is not a taboo subject, but something in which we can all be involved.

There have of course been many other television programmes which have touched on the subject of mental handicap, including series such as 'Let's Go', a weekly series for the mentally handicapped launched in 1981, and followed by a second series in 1983, and 'Accident of Birth', a series mainly for parents and people working with the mentally handicapped broadcast in early 1982.

In January 1983, BBC2's Man Alive showed a documentary called 'Only Time Would Tell' which discussed the life of Matthew Crosby, an 18 year old Down's teenager mainly through the eyes of his mother, Anne Crosby, who continues to believe that Matthew would have been better off dead and recalls her desire to end his life with a pillow a few days after his birth. Although the images of the film belied the opinions expressed within it ('unless the camera lied, Matthew appeared to be a loveable, reasonable, biddable child capable of enjoying life within its limits'[1]), the mood of the programme was that we could well be better without mentally handicapped people, who have an unsatisfactory life and require an unfair devotion of care.

Other general television programmes covering news events have been more sympathetic, and there are regular programmes on the radio which both discuss various aspects of mental handicap or refer to it.

Newspaper coverage of mental handicap remains curiously ambiguous. Many mentions of mental handicap in the press stem from coverage in other media (new books, plays, films etc) and thus take the form of criticism. Usually there is some implied opinion within such critiques, and this is generally a sympathetic one, so that such productions as 'Walter' were admired for their production values but questioned over their intent.

If the press is not reviewing other media, it is normally reporting on current events. In this sense, it can be of vital importance in expressing versions of events concerning the mentally handicapped.

The power of the media in this role reached a height during the Leonard Arthur case, when the *Daily Mail* published an article by

[1] *The Daily Telegraph* January 13th, 1983, Richard Last.

Malcolm Muggeridge about Mrs Marilyn Carr, a candidate in a Croydon by-election who was standing on a 'pro-life programme'; against abortion and the medical termination of babies born deformed or with Down's Syndrome. Mrs Carr had good reason to take such a stance as she had been born without arms.

The *Daily Mail,* or more specifically the Editor, David English, was taken to court because he had published the article during the Leonard Arthur case and was held in contempt of court. It was felt that such a strong 'right to live' article would prejudice the jury in the case.

Sadly, the case had more to do with the freedom of the press than with the rights of the mentally handicapped to live, and when the *Mail* was cleared of contempt by the Law Lords it was a victory for the freedom of the press not the mentally handicapped present in our society.

Nonetheless, papers such as the *Daily Mail* have been prominent in publishing articles and letters about mental handicap, and in particular in discussing the right to live issue. Undoubtedly in the case of the *Mail,* this policy stems from their strong middle class female readership profile, but other papers have also given regular space to mental handicap issues within what they see as a 'crusading' role towards the British public.

There have been few attempts to portray mental handicap in the theatre, and despite its progressive nature, the theatre has been slow to respond to the challenge on offer. Recent plays have focussed on the sensational, and probably the most successful recent depiction was in a play written over 100 years ago as a novel, the National Theatre's production of Nicholas Nickleby featuring the character, 'Smike'.

Perhaps the best known play, and eventual film, about mental handicap was 'A Day in the Death of Joe Egg' based on the true-life story of Abigail, born to the playwright Peter Nichols, and born a spastic due to a difficult birth. Nichols encountered difficulties in staging a play on what was at the time, circa 1967, a difficult and sensitive subject although the difficulties were compounded by the frank dialogue. Abigail was placed in permanent care at the age of three in a mental hospital where she remained until her death in 1971. Writing of her death (*The Observer,* May 1984), Nichols observed:

> "That afternoon the matron of Abigail's hospital rang from Bristol to tell us her lungs had finally got the better of her heart and she'd died an hour ago. We exchanged the necessary platitudes and I thanked her for her care. Thelma and Louise were both upset but I shed no tears over what we all knew was a happy event . . .
>
> ". . . I dare say everyone tried to remember Abo and her 11 empty years."

Again, the playwright plays the role, albeit true life role, of the thinking man's condemnation of mental handicap. And these final comments, addressed over the child's death, seem to justify themselves in the sense that the playwright is speaking not only from experience, but for all the parents who dread that this might happen to them. Yet for those who have cared for mentally handicapped children and seen them develop, must come doubts as to whether Peter Nichols, or Paula Milne, ever really gave their children a chance.

A typical recent example was the production 'Care' written by Roy Mitchell and shown at the Theatre Upstairs in February, 1983. The plot was described as follows by the theatre:

> "Terry and Cheryl met at school, married at 17 and live and work in their native Birmingham. Terry works at Longbridge, Cheryl at Dolcis. Together they have a Ford Escort, a colour television, a three piece suite, a cat and a problem that won't go away."

This coy introduction refers to a problem consisting of a 'vegetable' child who is kept locked away in a cupboard, and who they eventually kill. It remains highly questionable why such a sensational and unrealistic play should be thought worthy of attention in the first place, but this is perhaps indicative of attitudes within the theatre that mental handicap is a good basis for plays written by writers who have no understanding of mental handicap but view it as a subject of horror around which some dramatic scenario can be created.

Films have generally been few on the ground, perhaps the most successful being Ira Wohl's 'Best Boy' a documentary based on the life of his cousin, Philly, a 52 year old Down's person. A British film, 'Donal and Sally' fictionally presented the lives of two mentally handicapped people who fall in love and wish to marry. Although the film did not accurately portray the attitudes and feelings of mentally handicapped people, it may be commended for bringing a sensitive subject into the public eye.

The overall conclusion is that while there is no shortage of regular comment and coverage of mental handicap in the mass media, there have been few attempts over recent years to explore the subject in any depth, and those that have, have focussed on the sensational and the controversial. Yet the media offer the major — if not only—means by which the British public can understand more about mental handicap.

Above all, the key to understanding will come when the mentally handicapped are treated within normal life, rather than observed as subjects, in a sensational way. In this sense, the decision to incorporate a Down's Syndrome child in the series, 'Crossroads' must be strongly praised. For the first time, a mentally handicapped child has been built into a programme about normal people living in normal lives, rather than made the subject of a sensational film or documentary.

Overall, the dilemma between the accurate depiction of mental handicap and 'good television' will remain. The major television stations, in looking towards a mass audience, will inevitably focus on more dramatic events and issues in their depiction of the subject, and one's only hope is that such depictions will be balanced and sensitively written. There must always be the fear that, however good a writer may be involved, the depiction of mental handicap will be unrealistic because the writer will have no real understanding about the subject.

For the minor channels, and here we may include BBC2 and Channel Four, and may in the future add local cable stations, considerable opportunities exist to report on developments in the field of mental handicap. By accurate and sensible reporting, mirrored by intelligent coverage in the press and on the radio, the public could become much better informed about mental handicap and this increased awareness could have a tremendous impact on the ways that our mentally handicapped population are perceived in modern society. But there is a long way to go.

# CHAPTER EIGHT

# TOWARDS A BETTER UNDERSTANDING

This book has discussed the nature of mental handicap in Britain today, and the ways that attitudes to the mentally handicapped community are changing. Due, to a large extent, to the activities of the voluntary organisations, who have always been in the forefront in guiding policy on this issue, much has been achieved. In general a more liberal attitude prevails; more is known about the causes and nature of mental handicap, and how best to approach the problems of education and care.

The controversies surrounding severe mental handicap which began in the early 1980s sparked off a national debate which continues today. Such life or death issues are fundamental to our society, and the cases discussed in Chapter Six challenged long-established prerogatives held by the medical profession and by parents and families. That such cases brought a hitherto taboo subject into the open is a welcome sign that such a fundamental issue as a child's right to live will no longer be determined by small groups of people who through lack of a real knowledge of the subject may come to devastatingly wrong decisions.

Controversy, too, continues to surround the abortion issue. Women who have no objection to abortion in principle feel that it is entirely within their right to abort babies who have been diagnosed as being mentally handicapped; certainly at present there are few legal restraints, but there are practical as well as moral problems involved. As work continues to reduce the gestation period at which screening tests can be conducted, the practical problems will decrease. The final question will be a moral one: do we want to bring mentally handicapped children into the world?

Such a question would inevitably be negatively answered by the great majority of people. To change this attitude, if we assume for a moment that we would wish to change it, would either require a change in fundamental attitude or some form of new legislation. New laws protecting the mentally handicapped from conception to the early days of life would be strongly opposed an a breach of civil liberties, hence the generally adverse reaction to the bringing of the Leonard Arthur case, and the Hammersmith and Rochdale Down's cases. The public reaction was generally that parents and doctors should decide.

What would be desired, therefore, is a fundamental change in attitude among the British public to the whole subject of mental handicap. Such a change would be brought about by convincing the public that there is really no difference between people who are mentally handicapped and those who are not. On this basis, no parents would consider abortion for 'Reason Four' (see Chapter Five); everything possible would be done to help the survival of the severely handicapped; parents would in almost all cases wish to keep their child, and there would be no actual difference between bringing up a child who was mentally handicapped and one who was not, or one who was disabled or one who was not, unless the necessary support services were lacking.

The logic of this change in attitude is expressed in educational terms in the Warnock Report, the findings of which have now been incorporated into the Education Act. The report rejected the idea of two distinct groups of children, the handicapped and the non-handicapped, of whom the former had special education and the latter just education. The assumption made was that perhaps as many as one child in five might need special educational help at some stage in their school career. Efforts should therefore be made to integrate handicapped children into the normal educational process, exempting children with distinct disabilities who greatly benefit from special, perhaps private education.

If this notion of integration were developed within our total society, the mentally handicapped would cease to be regarded as a race apart. We have already discussed how the policy of segregating the mentally handicapped in long stay hospitals is being abandoned to be replaced by more widespread fostering in tandem with short term care, and the use of group homes in ordinary houses and ordinary streets. Such changes are extending the policy of integration beyond the confines of the educational system to the way that mentally handicapped people live their lives.

Such changes are, however, being implemented by people who have the needs of the mentally handicapped at heart. The vast majority of the British public, although generally sympathetic to the problems, maintain stubborn and inflexible attitudes to the subject of mental handicap, especially if the problems intrude into their lives. Only when the barriers of ignorance and fear are destroyed will our mentally handicapped community be fully integrated into our society, and decisions and judgements—perhaps of a life or death nature—be made with a full and real understanding of the issues involved.

One of the most frequent reactions to the observation that many people do not understand about mental handicap is to question why they should. People tend to assume that parents of mentally handicapped children and those who work with them are gifted with abnormal powers of patience and understanding, or suffused with some form of religious or social awareness that make them adopt a sacrificial purpose in life. In practice, they are just ordinary people who for some reason—and the reason is often accidental—have become involved with the mentally handicapped. If they have since discovered that this contact can be fulfilling and life-enhancing—and this is certainly not always the case—it is because they have benefitted from the broader range of experiences which this contact has offered. In the great majority of cases, their attitudes to the mentally handicapped will have changed as a result of experiencing this broader perspective. Yet many people who work with the mentally handicapped find it depressing, difficult and unfulfilling. In that sense, it is like any other job of work, or like being any parent.

People who doubt that they would be able to cope with a mentally handicapped child express a completely understandable point of view. They will probably not have spent any amount of time with a mentally handicapped person or really know how they behave. Their contact will probably have been very superficial, and immediate reactions, especially on meeting severely handicapped people for the first time, ones of alarm. In addition, people are influenced by their own preconceptions, which will have evolved, in all but the very young, in far less enlightened times. Compounding these fears, based on little but public ignorance, is the concept of mental handicap conveyed through the mass media, with such films as 'Walter' portraying the lives of the mentally handicapped as being harrowing and filled with despair.

This sense of wariness and unease permeates our society, and will remain a barrier both to parents accepting mentally handicapped children, and to the public at large accepting them within our society. Yet everyone may come into contact with the mentally handicapped at some stage in their lives; indeed any one of us may be accidentally brain damaged. It is an immediate issue for us all.

Such an involvement, with its need for a clear and sensible understanding, may begin when screening tests reveal that the child a woman is carrying may be handicapped. Under present conditions, time will be short; the parents will be advised of the risks and consequences of their actions, but it will be stressed that they must decide. On what basis will this decision be made?

Most books which have been written about mental handicap are for doctors, nurses, parents with mentally handicapped children, social workers; rarely for the general public. The knowledge which the parents possess will be based on perhaps a superficial understanding built up over many years and based largely on misconceptions. Television documentaries have tended to play on the more harrowing aspects of the subject, rather than the normal day-to-day lives. The decision will probably be made on little evidence, and will probably be towards an abortion, even if the child might be desperately wanted and the parents generally against abortion in principle.

What will the doctor advise? The advice could vary greatly because medical opinion is deeply divided over this issue and many doctors have the same lack of understanding as the general public. An ability to help bring a child into the world and care for it does not necessarily create a good parent.

The doctor may thus be positive or negative. If the latter, how will they present the facts; that the child will probably not live very long;

may have an 'unhappy' life; will need constant supervision and care; be perhaps better off unborn? If the advice is more positive, will the parents be able to shrug off attitudes which have built up over decades in a few days?

Only if would-be parents fully understand about mental handicap can they make the right sort of rational decisions when faced with these circumstances and face the situation with a true sense of proportion. If their attitudes are based on ignorance and fear, they will be unable to make a balanced judgement if the problem arises.

This is equally crucial once the child has been born. If the baby is severely handicapped, they may be involved in a discussion over whether the child should be allowed to die. If the baby survives, they will have to decide whether they want to keep the child, and here there is more time for consideration. But despite the positive counselling they may well receive, many parents, especially fathers, find it impossible to come to terms with the nature of their son or daughter. This overwhelming sense of rejection is based on dreading this prospect all their lives, and difficult to change and undermine in weeks or even months.

But it is not just prospective parents who have contact with mentally handicapped people, and the attitudes of many people in positions of authority are crucial in that they will make decisions which will affect the lives of our mentally handicapped community.

Potential employers, for example, have to weigh up the possibilities of employing mentally handicapped people; schoolteachers and heads may have to accommodate handicapped children in normal schools; members of a jury may have to pass verdict on a mildly handicapped person. Doctors and nurses may have to make crucial decisions over newly born children, and hoteliers, retailers and café proprietors are in a position to make decisions which will affect the freedom of mentally handicapped people to live their lives.

It is not enough, therefore, to set aside these issues as being the concern of others. Only when the public comes to a fuller understanding of the place of the mentally handicapped in our society, and appreciates what mentally handicapped people are really like and what they can achieve, will real progress be made in their integration back into the society of which they are a part.

Information on the nature of public attitudes to mental handicap came to light in a survey conducted for MENCAP in March 1982 by MORI (Market & Opinion Research International). The survey was based on a sample of 2,000 interviews. One question in the survey concerned the emotional responses of people to the mentally handicapped. Of the sample, 70% expressed feelings of sympathy and 51% sadness; 31% were worried about coping with them, and 71% felt unease with them. The public is not therefore antagonistic towards the mentally handicapped or especially afraid of them; the emotional responses are generally to feel sorry for them and uncomfortable in their presence.

---

**EMOTIONAL RESPONSES TO THE MENTALLY HANDICAPPED**

Which of the following best describe your feelings towards the mentally handicapped?

| | |
|---|---|
| Sympathy | 70% |
| Sadness | 51 |
| Acceptance | 49 |
| Friendliness | 46 |
| Kindness | 45 |
| Worry about coping with them | 31 |
| At ease with them | 29 |
| Confident about coping with them | 17 |
| Discomfort | 14 |
| Embarrassment | 13 |
| Fear of them | 4 |
| Indifference | 3 |
| Anger | 1 |
| Dislike | neg |

Source: MORI/MENCAP survey 1982

A further question from the MORI—MENCAP survey, asked what the public attitudes would be to mentally handicapped adults

## CONCERNS ABOUT MENTALLY HANDICAPPED NEIGHBOURS

If two mentally handicapped adults moved in next door to you, would the following be a major concern, a minor concern or no concern at all?

| | Major Concern % | Minor Concern % | No Concern % | No Opinion % | Total* % |
|---|---|---|---|---|---|
| They might not get enough professional care | 38 | 35 | 22 | 5 | 100 |
| Local people/children might make fun of them | 38 | 44 | 15 | 3 | 100 |
| They might feel isolated | 28 | 40 | 26 | 6 | 100 |
| They might harm local children/police | 20 | 26 | 50 | 5 | 100 |
| You may have to help look after them | 12 | 32 | 51 | 6 | 100 |
| They might harm pets | 10 | 21 | 63 | 6 | 100 |
| You would miss the company of normal neighbours | 10 | 22 | 65 | 4 | 100 |
| They might damage property | 8 | 29 | 59 | 5 | 100 |
| You might feel awkward in their presence | 7 | 34 | 55 | 4 | 100 |
| They might cause noise/disturbance | 8 | 35 | 53 | 4 | 100 |
| Your home could lose value | 7 | 17 | 70 | 6 | 100 |
| Children might become friendly with them | 5 | 18 | 72 | 5 | 100 |
| Friends might avoid visiting you | 4 | 16 | 76 | 4 | 100 |
| You would be afraid to leave your home | 3 | 11 | 82 | 4 | 100 |

Source: MENCAP/MORI survey 1982 *Allow for rounding

moving into a house next door to them. The question was designed to establish the level of public concern over this development, so there were no positive suggestions, but the low concern rate for most of the problems posed suggested that the majority of people were not worried about this prospect, nor that it would trouble them personally, socially or financially to any great extent. The main concern was that it would not be ideal for the mentally handicapped people themselves, rather than prove an inconvenience or embarrassment to the respondents.

There is again therefore a sympathetic attitude running through these findings, with some uncertainty about the danger element, but no outright antagonism or opposition to the possibilities.

Other questions posed in the survey showed that:

- — 61% of the sample would be not at all concerned if a mentally handicapped child was allowed to attend the same school as their child
- — 63% think that mentally handicapped people should be allowed to marry
- — 47% of the above felt that they should be allowed to have children
- — 62% felt that they should be cared for in the community in ordinary homes rather than in special homes or hospitals
- — 50% thought that they should be looked after by social services rather than hospitals, with 34% opting for hospitals.

Although these proportions are not as high as many would like to see, the survey certainly did not reveal marked antagonism within society to the current developments on behalf of our mentally handicapped community. Nevertheless, if we adjust the above findings, they suggest that almost 40% of the public feel that mentally handicapped people should be segregated from the rest of society; around the same proportion would dislike the idea of a mentally handicapped child being at the same school as their child and around 70% feel that mentally handicapped people should not be allowed to marry and have children. Thus although the general attitude of the public is sympathetic to the mentally handicapped in our society, there remains an overriding sense of pity that they are as they are, and a feeling that there has to be some degree of segregation between them and the rest of society.

The underlying attitude is perhaps that most people accept mentally handicapped people and are sympathetic towards them, but remain inwardly glad that it has not happened to them or to their children —'there but for the grace of God, go I.' They also continue to believe the many myths surrounding the handicapped which have been passed on for decades.

It is said that mentally handicapped people do not normally enjoy a happy life. Whilst it is true that some mentally handicapped people suffer distress, this is equally true of other people in society. There is no substance in the assumption that because people are mentally handicapped they are less likely than anyone else to be happy.

People believe that there is a strong dividing line between the mentally handicapped and the 'normal'. In fact, there is no division and social and academic skills and abilities differ widely. The mentally handicapped are not a homogenous group to be sectioned off and segregated from everyone else. The concept of 'normality' has no real meaning other than that of the personal viewpoint of any individual. Because certain people do not conform to academic expectations or social abilities of others, this cannot place them outside society.

It is said that they place great strains on family life, and people feel they would be unable to cope with a mentally handicapped child. Yet as those who have had families know, raising any children is an activity which causes considerable problems, and given the full support of social services, short term care and essential back-up facilities services, most parents are able to cope and derive considerable fulfilment from their achievements.

It is said that mentally handicapped people die young. Although certain forms of severe mental handicap can lead to a limited life-expectancy, medical skills are improving considerably; for example, it is common for Down's adults to live into their fifties and sixties.

It is said that as mentally handicapped people cannot care for themselves, they will be left lonely and isolated when the parents are dead. But today, considerable strides are being made in the teaching and care of even the severely mentally handicapped, so that they are learning to do far more for themselves. Many can go on to lead virtually independent lives in 'core and cluster' schemes even if the handicap is severe, so that ideally the handicapped person would leave home to live independently after leaving school. It is wrong to assume that mentally handicapped people would, or should, remain at home into adulthood.

Undoubtedly many of the apprehensions about mental handicap stem from the nature of modern society with its emphasis on achieving and competition. Parents strive to ensure that their children are placed in the best possible schools, follow with avid interest their educational attainments, often placing the children under great pressure if they are relatively unsuccessful. On reaching adulthood, people continue to strive to be better than others; to earn more money, buy a larger home, hold down an interesting and fulfilling job and lead a rewarding life. Eventually, they too seek achievements in their own children.

Within this social spiral, and in a hard and competitive world, the mentally handicapped community are viewed as objects of pity; people who are not achieving; the stuff of charities and benevolence. People feel that they do not have much of a life, because in their terms, their lives seem unfulfilling and pointless.

But mentally handicapped people can achieve within their own terms. Their achievements may be limited when compared with those of others, but they are no less real and fulfilling for the people concerned.

Thus parents, employers and decision-makers have an obligation to have a full understanding of mental handicap in order to approach the issues involved with a true sense of proportion.

This will become increasingly important as efforts continue to integrate mentally handicapped people into the society of which they are a part, to reverse the policy of segregation begun in the last century. Plans to bring mentally handicapped people into ordinary streets will be thwarted by adverse public reaction unless efforts begin to educate the public about life with the mentally handicapped.

Such a process of education must inevitably commence with the young. Schools should be implementing courses to teach young people about mental handicap as these will be tomorrow's parents and neighbours.

Perhaps because the mind is the crucial organ in the human body, there has always been a tendency to ostracize such people from society. The efforts being made now to change these attitudes are seeking to reverse a trend which persisted for most of this century endorsed by official government attitudes to the care of the handicapped.

The differences between mental illness and mental handicap are widely known, yet legislation on the subject has consistently failed to take these differences into account. Successive governments continue to describe the disabled and handicapped as if they constitute an entity. In fact, one in 10 people in this country have some kind of disability and it is pointless to consider 5.5 million people as a separately identifiable group.

Yet it is not unusual to find that many people make no distinction between even the physically and the mentally handicapped, often to the apparent detriment of the former who have more capable brains. In fact, this is really to the detriment of the mentally handicapped who fall lower in public esteem as a result. It has made physically handicapped people keen to stress that they are not mentally handicapped, not stupid.

Undoubtedly, public acceptance of the physically handicapped will be easier to achieve. People are keen to applaud the successes of physically handicapped people who gain successful academic qualifications, and acquire practical skills. They find it harder to appreciate the successes of the mentally handicapped because they do not conform to their concept of success.

It is often maintained that mentally handicapped people are a burden on society. Certainly they make demands on social and medical services, and it is possible that severely mentally handicapped people will have to be looked after for all their lives. If the parents reject the child, this care will have to be provided by the state. No-one would maintain, however, that those of us who are unable to contribute economically to society through no fault of our own, should be denied our rights to live in society and derive its benefits.

Many people in our society place demands upon it. In a Christian society, it is a fundamental principle that people help each other, and that the stronger and the wealthier have an obligation to help the weaker and the poorer. Although it will never attain real equality, a democratic society will seek to ensure that there is a redistribution in wealth through taxation which funds the services which provide help to those that need it.

Yet we cannot describe the contributions made to society purely in economic terms, nor can we operate prejudices against any sector of society because the people involved do not conform to our concept of a normal life. Our society is built on interdependence, we all give to it, and take from it.

If a process of real integration is to occur, the British public must therefore gain a fuller understanding of the nature of mental handicap. How might this be achieved?

The attitudes of adults to the mentally handicapped tend to be firmly entrenched, and because many of the issues involved are emotive, these attitudes are difficult to change. Younger people are less susceptible to these prejudices and it is in the field of education that most can be achieved.

Mentally handicapped children should be given the opportunity of mixing with other children from an early age. Apart from the considerable advantages for the mentally handicapped child, the other children will have first hand contact with mental handicap at an early age. In the course of time, this contact will cease to have special significance, and the mentally handicapped child will just be another child.

For the same reason, handicapped children should be increasingly integrated into normal schools, although special schools will still be required for special learning difficulties. In addition to this process of educational integration, secondary schools should maintain close contact with special schools so that teenage children understand more about mental handicap. Just as they are taught other subjects, they should increasingly be taught about such topics as mental handicap so that they do not grow up with the prejudices that their parents may possess. The children should be given the opportunity to mix with handicapped people, and encouraged to participate in voluntary activities, helping in homes and at social clubs for the handicapped.

The media could also do much more to help people to understand about mental handicap. Although there have been some useful television series, most television coverage focusses on the sensational, and some major documentaries and plays have compounded the fears and misunderstandings of the public rather than alleviate them. The very way that news stories and programmes about mental handicap are reported falls into the same trap of assuming that the whole subject is sad and despairing, mainly because the journalists and broadcasters possess the same lack of understanding as their viewers. Due to their crusading streak, newspapers have been valuable in discussing the achievements of the mentally handicapped, but again they tend to focus on the sensational.

Possibly the most significant development in television history in its depiction of the mentally handicapped occurred in 1983 when a mentally handicapped child was written into the television soap opera, 'Crossroads', which has a viewing audience of 14 million. The child 'star' was a six-year old Down's girl called Nina. It was thought by the producers that the programme slipped out of the top ten ratings for a few weeks because of the squeamishness of some viewers, but this was probably just a seasonal fluctuation. It soon climbed back.

The 'Crossroads' experiment presented a mentally handicapped child within the dimensions of a programme which purports to be about real people and real life, and to explore some of the issues raised in having such a child. The producer of the programme, Jack Barton, felt that "if the viewers could accept Nina and her disabilities, there was a chance of chipping away at some of the old prejudices that stand to prevent mentally handicapped people from being accepted in the community."[1]

1 'How reality came to Crossroads', *The Guardian,* December 2nd, 1983.

If there could be more attempts like this to show mentally handicapped lives in their normality, rather than in a sensational way, the media could play a major role in helping the public to understand more about the lives that handicapped people lead; that they are not all anguish and broken dreams, but often constructive, fulfilling and as life enhancing as anyone else's.

It will take years for a real process of integration to take place, possibly generations. But as work continues to undo the errors of the past in the care and treatment of the mentally handicapped and plan for the future, efforts must now begin to re-educate the public and dispell the misconceptions which still abound in our society even among its higher echelons.

The Office of Health Economics highlighted this very issue in *Mental Handicap: Ways Forward,* published in 1978:

> "One of the more unfortunate effects of segregated institutional care is that it encourages 'ordinary' members of the population to think of 'the handicapped' as a race apart. Mentally handicapped individuals become strangers even within their own families. Thus it is not surprising that other people tend to underestimate their abilities and personal qualities.
>
> "For example, a decreasing number of persons still object to locally based provisions for mentally handicapped people because understandably their picture of the latter is bounded by bizarre and frightening images often associated with traditional mental handicap hospitals . . . Such prejudice will fade as new patterns of care are established, bringing more mentally handicapped people into open contact with the general public. It is to be hoped that as this happens, the mass media will switch away from the valuable role of exposing the horrors of the past to the more challenging and difficult one of discussing mental handicap in the context of normal day to day life."

In summarising some of the major developments in the case of the mentally handicapped in 1981, Peter Mittler wrote:—

> "Like all fellow citizens, they have a right to:—
>
> — be taught by appropriately trained teachers in settings that encourage the maximum of contact with other children
>
> — a home of their own, in an ordinary house with as much help and support as their individual needs demand

— work, which is meaningful, satisfying and paid

— full access without discrimination to the whole range of services and leisure opportunities available to the rest of the community

— make friends and develop a relationship with the opposite sex."

In addition, mentally handicapped people have a right to expect people to understand them and accept them within the society of which they are a part; a right to be born and a right to live.

# APPENDIX A:

# FURTHER READING

Many books have been written about mental handicap. The following list is intended as a brief guide to some of the more basic sources of information available, including the primary governmental assessments. The publications are available through Her Majesty's Stationery Offices or from the Mencap Bookshop, at 123 Golden Lane, London EC1 which has a comprehensive range of relevant publications on mental handicap.

**Better Services for the Mentally Handicapped**

A key paper setting out policy plans for the care of the mentally handicapped during the 1970s with targets to 1990.

*Department of Health and Social Security/Welsh Office, 1971 £1.50*

**Mental Handicap: Progress, Problems and Priorities**

A review of mental handicap services in England since the 1971 White Paper.

*Department of Health and Social Security, 1980*

**A Better Life: Report on Services for the Mentally Handicapped in Scotland**

*Scottish Home and Health Department/Scottish Education Department 1979 £2.50*

**Special Educational Needs: Report of the Committee of Enquiry into the Education of Handicapped Children and Young People**

The influential Warnock report which set out new plans for educating mentally handicapped children in the 1980s.

*HMSO 1978 £6.65*

**Report of the Committee of Enquiry into Mental Handicap Nursing and Care**

The Peggy Jay report, published in two volumes and offering both a useful insight into the subject of mental handicap and an in-depth assessment of current standards of nursing and care.

*HMSO 1979 £3.00*

**Mental Handicap: Ways Forward**

A perceptive overall assessment of mental handicap.

*Office of Health Economics, 1978 35p*

**Birth Impairments**

A further useful pamphlet about congenital malformations.

*Office of Health Economics, 1978 35p*

**Accident of Birth: Aspects of Mental Handicap**

An introduction to the subject of mental handicap by Fred Heddel, written in conjunction with the BBC series of the same name and considering some recent pilot schemes for the care and education of the mentally handicapped.

*BBC, 1982 £0.00*

**Preventing of Mental Handicap**

A series of papers based on conference proceedings and concerning various types of preventive techniques.

*British Institute of Mental Handicap, 1979*

**Mental Handicap in the Eighties**

An appraisal of general trends in the care of the mentally handicapped written in the International Year of the Disabled. With contributions by Joan Bicknell, Judy Fryd, Alan and Ann Clarke and Peter Mittler.

*Mencap, 1981 £1.00*

**Elements of a Comprehensive Local Service for People with Mental Handicap**

A significant statement of key aims by the major voluntary organisations concerned in mental handicap.

*Independent Development Council for People with Mental Handicap, 1982*

**Genetic Counselling**

A pamphlet about genetic counselling for the mentally handicapped by Brian Kirman.

*Mencap 1981 50p*

**Down's Syndrome: a short account of the condition known as mongolism**

by Ludwig Lowenstein

*Mencap, 1981 50p*

**Down's Syndrome: Let's Be Positive**

A report by J R Ludlow on the teaching and training of Down's Syndrome children.

*Down's Children Association, 1980*

**The Genetics of Down's Syndrome (An Account for Parents)**

A report by M d'A Crawford explaining the genetic origins of Down's Syndrome and the preventive methods available.

*Down's Children Association, 1980*

**Public Attitudes towards the Mentally Handicapped**

A consumer survey by MORI into public attitudes

*Mencap, 1982 £1.50*

# APPENDIX B

# MEDIA COVERAGE

**Feature Films Concerned with Mental Handicap**
(Available for hire)

| | |
|---|---|
| *Best Boy* (1979) | Documentary by Ira Wohl on his mentally handicapped cousin Philly, aged 52. Philly has spent most of his life with his parents; the film follows his going out into the world as his parents age and die. |
| *Bunny* (Thames TV 1972) | A film by the parents of Bunny, a 5-year-old child with brain damage who has unsuccessful brain surgery in the UK, but who is operated on successfully in the USA. The film observes Bunny's progress through the post-operative treatment in America, and shows how this method of treatment affected his parents' lives. |
| *Donal and Sally* (1979) | A 75 minute play in which two mentally handicapped young people fall in love at a training centre in Scotland. Discussions between parents and teachers explore their right to love and marry and the dangers inherent in them. |
| *The Spongers* (BBC TV 1978) | A play about a mother with four children, one of whom suffers from Down's Syndrome. The family fights for its rights, and loses. The handicapped child was played by a Down's Syndrome actress. |

| | |
|---|---|
| *Stepping Out* (1979) | Made for Australian television, the film documents the preparation and performance of a dance entertainment by a group of mentally handicapped people, at Sydney Opera House. |

All these films are available for hire from:
Concord Films Council
201 Felixstowe Road
Ipswich
Suffolk. Tel: (0473) 76012/715754

A catalogue of films dealing with mental handicap is published by the Mental Health Film Council,
22 Harley Street
London W1N 2ED Tel: 01-637 0741

## Television Broadcasts on Mental Handicap from 1981—February 1984

| | | |
|---|---|---|
| 11 Jan '82 onwards | *Let's Go (Series)*<br>Weekly series for young, mentally handicapped people, designed to teach them social skills. | BBC 1 |
| 23 Jan '81 | *Scene: James Is Our Brother*<br>Film about a 16-year-old boy with Down's Syndrome, and his life and family. At the end, the boy, now 22, brings his story up to date. | BBC 1 |
| 17 Feb '81 | *Return to Life*<br>Documentary about the Turner Village Hospital's methods of rehabilitating the mentally handicapped in the community. | BBC 1 |

| | | |
|---|---|---|
| 18 Feb '81 | *Grapevine (Series)*<br>Report on an action group in Edinburgh which runs a centre for mentally handicapped people. | BBC 2 |
| 10 Jun '81 | *Silent Minority*<br>Documentary report on the treatment of mentally handicapped people in hospitals. The emphasis was on the distressing conditions arising from lack of staff and funds, and provoked a strong public reaction. | ITV (Central) |
| 11 Jun '81 | *Thames Report (Series)*<br>Report on mentally handicapped children. | ITV (Thames) |
| 24 Jun '81 | *I Was At Broadmoor*<br>Documentary report on treatment of Broadmoor patients, seen through the eyes of an ex-patient and ex-staff. | ITV (Central) |
| 19 Jul '81 | *Link (Series)*<br>General report on mental handicap. | ITV (Central) |
| 24 Jul '81 to 4 Sept '81 | *One In A Hundred (Series)*<br>A series of 7 programmes reporting on recent changes in thinking about mental handicap. | ITV (Scottish (TV) |
| 28 Jul '81 | *James Is Our Brother*<br>Repeat. | BBC 2 |
| 8 Sept '81 | *Medical Express (Series)*<br>Report on an 11-year-old child suffering from the rare Prader Willi disease, which makes him mentally handicapped and gives him an insatiable appetite, though he needs few calories. His mother has started a Prader Willi Parents' Association. | BBC 1 |

| | | |
|---|---|---|
| 3 Oct '81 | *Maureen*<br>A dramatised documentary about a day in the life of an epileptic, mentally handicapped patient at Northgate Hospital, Morpeth. | BBC 2 |
| 5 Oct '81 | *Land 'n' Larder*<br>Report on two centres for the mentally handicapped, Glencraig and Mournegrange, which are involved in agriculture. | BBC 1 (Northern Ireland) |
| 12 Oct '81 onwards | *Let's Go (Series)*<br>Repeat. | BBC 1 |
| 22 Oct '81 | *Forty Minutes (Series)*<br>Report on the public hearing which decided whether 618 patients in Calderstone Mental Handicap Hospital should be entitled to the vote. | BBC 2 |
| 21 Dec '81 | *Nationwide (Series)*<br>Investigated St Lawrence's mental hospital. | BBC 1 |
| 31 Dec '81 | *The Ravenswood Experience*<br>Documentary about a private Berkshire village which offers lifelong residential care to mentally handicapped people. | ITV (Thames) |
| 2 Jan '82 | *The Ravenswood Experience*<br>Repeat. | ITV (Thames) |
| | *Accident of Birth (Series for parents and those working with the mentally handicapped)* | BBC 1 |
| 10 Jan '82 | What is Mental Handicap? | |
| 17 Jan '82 | Long Stay Hospitals | |
| 24 Jan '82 | Special Education | |
| 31 Jan '82 | Education and Training | |

| | | |
|---|---|---|
| 7 Feb '82 | The Swedish System | |
| 14 Feb '82 | What Kind of Future? | |
| 18 Feb '82 | *Current Account: the Ark—A Family Home*<br>Report on a home for mentally handicapped adults. | BBC 1 (Scotland) |
| 22 Mar '82 | *World In Action (Series)*<br>Report on treating mentally handicapped people in hospitals. | ITV (Granada) |
| Apr '82 and May '82 | *Horace (Series)*<br>Drama series about a 40-year-old man with a mental age of 10, who lives with his mother. Barry Jackson played Horace. The series was generally admired for sensitivity and a light touch. | ITV (Yorkshire TV) |
| 5 May '82 | *Where There's Life (Series)*<br>Interviews with the parents of mentally handicapped children. | ITV (Yorkshire TV) |
| 21 Jul '82 | Report on the possibilities of plastic surgery for Down's Syndrome sufferers. | ITV (Yorkshire TV) |
| 24 Oct '82 | *Credo (Series)*<br>Report on mentally handicapped patients in closed institutions. Examines how the passing of the Mental Health Act is likely to worsen a problematic situation. | ITV (London Weekend TV) |

| | | |
|---|---|---|
| 12 Nov '82 | *Our Winnie*<br>Play by Alan Bennett about a mentally handicapped girl being taken on a 'treat' by her mother. The mother (Elizabeth Spriggs) has always had to fight to come to terms with Winnie's handicap. | BBC 2 |
| 13 Nov '82 | *Walter*<br>A film, adapted from the book by David Cook, about a mentally handicapped man who is admitted to a hospital when his parents die. Ian McKellen played Walter: his acting, and the play as a whole (directed by Stephen Frears) were widely acclaimed. | Channel 4 |
| 23 Nov '82 | *John David*<br>A play, based on a true story, about the birth of a Down's Syndrome child, and his parents' rejection of him. Paula Milne wrote the play, and the book from which it was adapted, and was the child's mother in real life. | BBC 1 |
| 16 Dec '82 | *Best Boy*<br>A documentary drama about Philly, a mentally handicapped man of 52 who has spent almost all his life with his parents. The film follows his leaving home, as his parents age and die, and his attempts to find independence. Directed by Ira Wohl. | Channel 4 |
| 9 Jan '83 | *Let's Go (Series)*<br>New series, produced by Charles Pascoe. | BBC 1 |

| | | |
|---|---|---|
| 13 Jan '83 | *Only Time Would Tell* Documentary on MacIntyre residential school for mentally handicapped children, and the life of one Down's Syndrome child there, and that of his parents. | BBC 2 |
| 9 Mar '83 onwards | *Chip's Comic (Series)* A series for children, helping them with early learning, with especial reference to mentally handicapped and ESN children, and the age range catered for is 3-10 years. | Channel 4 |
| 15 May '83 | *Link (Series)* Report on the rights of mental patients. | ITV (Central) |
| 26 May '83 | *Walter and June* The sequel film to *Walter*. In this, Walter falls in love and leaves the institution to live with June. Taken from David Cook's book, 'Winter Doves'. | Channel 4 |
| 10 Jul '83 | *Silent Minority* Repeat of the ITV-Central documentary on mental hospitals. | Channel 4 |
| 14 Aug '83 | *Children Out of Mind* Report on the teaching of physically and mentally handicapped children. | ITV (London Weekend TV) |
| 25 Aug '83 | *Link (Series) : Help Special* 'Home Is This'—a report on hospitals for the mentally handicapped, which examines how many of the patients should really be there. | ITV (Thames) |

| | | |
|---|---|---|
| | *I'm Young But Special (Series)* | ITV (Scottish TV) |
| 7 Nov '83 | Report on children with special needs. | |
| 14 Nov '83 | Report on behavioural and emotional problems of mentally handicapped children. | |
| 21 Nov '83 | Report on mentally handicapped children in schools and training units. | |
| 9 Nov '83 | *20-20 Vision (Series) : The Quiet Crisis* Report on caring for elderly relatives, including a consideration of senile dementia. | Channel 4 |
| Nov '83 and Dec '83 | *Crossroads (drama series)* A young Down's Syndrome girl arrives at the Crossroads motel after her mother has a nervous breakdown. Nina Weill, in real-life a Down's Syndrome sufferer, took the part. Her role lasted 6 weeks and caused a huge audience response and press interest—mainly favourable although there were some objections. | ITV |
| 20 Nov '83 onwards | *People First (Series)* 5 part series for the parents of mentally handicapped children. | BBC 1 |
| 3 Jan '84 | *First Tuesday (Series)* *Summer Holiday/Goodbye Joey:* Documentary film about the holiday taken by a group of mentally handicapped people in Teignmouth, where many of the local hoteliers and traders objected to their presence. | ITV (Yorkshire TV) |
| Jan '84 | *Emmerdale Farm (Drama Series)* An autistic child arrives in the neighbourhood. | ITV (Yorkshire TV) |

| | | |
|---|---|---|
| (Scheduled Sept '84) | *Chip's Comic (Series)* New series of learning programmes. | Channel 4 |

**Recently Published Novels Dealing With Mental Handicap**

*John David* by Paula Milne — Virago Press

The author's true story of giving birth to a baby with Down's Syndrome, and rejecting it. The book analyses the reactions of the parents and their friends and families to the dilemma and their decision.

*Simple Simon* by Ann Lovell — Lion Books

A true story about bringing up an autistic child, the breakdown it caused to the parents' marriage and the mother's altered outlook on life as a result of the experience.

*Walter* by David Cook — Penguin Books

A prize-winning novel about a mentally handicapped man who is admitted to an institution on his parents' death. The narrative is Walter's own.

*Winter Doves* by David Cook — Penguin Books

The Sequel to *Walter,* in which Walter falls in love and leaves the institution to try to make a life in the outside world with his lover, June.

**Theatre**—Recent Productions Concerned with Mental Handicap

| | | | |
|---|---|---|---|
| *Silent Screaming*<br>by Val Smith | Barnes Theatre Group | end 1980/<br>early 1981 | |
| *Care*<br>by Roy Mitchell<br>Dir: Antonia Bird | Theatre Upstairs<br>Royal Court | February | 1983 |
| | A sombre portrayal of the lives of Terry (Peter Hugo-Daly) and Cheryl (Gwyneth Strong), a young married couple with a severely brain-damaged child. They cannot cope, keep the child hidden in a cupboard and eventually kill it. | | |
| *Not Much to Ask* | The Graeae Company | | |
| At: | The Riverside Studios, London | 18-20 Nov | 1983 |
| | York Arts Centre, York | 22-26 Nov | 1983 |
| | West End Centre, Aldershot | 9 Dec | 1983 |
| | Immarsh College of PE, Liverpool | 12-19 Dec | 1983 |
| | A satire on institutional care, based loosely on Charlotte Bronte's novel, Villette. A production by the Graeae, a company composed of disabled actors. | | |

| | | | |
|---|---|---|---|
| *He'll Have To Go* | The Strathcona Company | | |
| At: | The Cottesloe, National Theatre, London | 6 Nov | 1983 |
| Directors:<br>Janet Bliss<br>Joan Greening<br>Mark Thompson<br>all of the<br>Strathcona Centre | A show developed and performed by 26 mentally handicapped actors, students of the Strathcona Social Education and Training Centre, Brent. The show included dance and music and was based on the actors' personal feelings and experiences. | | |

**Regular Radio Programmes For and About Mentally Handicapped People**

| *Time of Broadcast* | *Title and Description of Programme* | *Radio Station* (& Contact) |
|---|---|---|
| Mon 3-5pm | *Advice Lines*<br>Off-air confidential advice service: disability & mental health on alternate weeks. | *BBC Radio London*<br>Gloria Abramoff |
| Weekdays<br>8.10-8.30am | *Aithris Na Maidne*<br>Programme including information for mentally handicapped people. | *BBC Radio Nan Eilean*<br>Allan MacDoland |
| Tue-Fri 12-4pm<br>Sat 10am-2pm | *Artsline*<br>Confidential telephone information service for disabled and handicapped people wishing to be involved in the arts, as spectators or performers. | *Capital Radio*<br>Marilyn Pettman |
| Wed 8.30-9pm | *Challenge*<br>Programme for handicapped people. | *Red Rose Radio*<br>Keith Macklin |
| Mon 6.06-6.30pm | *Contact*<br>Produced by and for disabled people. | *CBC*<br>Tony Charles |

| | | |
|---|---|---|
| Fri 7.05pm | *Contact*<br>Includes items of interest to handicapped people | *BBC Radio Merseyside*<br>Margaret Roberts |
| Weekdays 12.45pm | *DevonCare*<br>Information advice, including features for the mentally handicapped. | *DevonAir Radio*<br>Gerri Jutsam |
| Sat 4.30-5pm | *Does He Take Sugar?*<br>Programme for and with disabled and handicapped people. | *BBC Radio 4*<br>Marlene Pease |
| Sun 8.30am | *Graham Ledger's Breakfast Show*<br>Includes a what's on feature for handicapped people. | *Radio 210*<br>Marion Fountayne |
| Regular broadcasts | *Handicapped & Disabled Information*<br>Public service announcements, voiced by local people. | *Radio Trent*<br>Len Groat |
| Mon 6.30pm | *Helping Hand*<br>Magazine Programme for handicapped people. | *Downtown Radio*<br>Alan Ferguson |
| Tue & Thur 3.20pm | *Sussex Afternoon*<br>Includes news for handicapped people. | *Southern Sound*<br>Andrew Winter |

# APPENDIX C:

# SUMMARY OF AVAILABLE STATISTICS

This section presents some basic statistics on mental handicap in Britain, mainly referring to England and Wales. Some brief comments are appended.

Tables

**Table 1**
**PREVALENCE RATES FOR MENTAL HANDICAP: SUMMARY OF CASE STUDIES**

Rates per 1,000 inhabitants

| | Age Group | Mental Handicap | Severe Mental Handicap | Down's Syndrome |
|---|---|---|---|---|
| England & Wales (urban) 1925-7 | 7-14 | 20.9 | 3.71 | 0.34 |
| Middlesex 1960 | 5-9 | 30.1 | | |
| | 7-14 | | 3.45 | 1.14 |
| | 10-14 | 36.1 | 3.61 | |
| Salford 1961 | 5-9 | 19.8 | | |
| | 10-14 | 28.4 | | |
| | 15-19 | | 3.62 | 0.9 |
| Aberdeen 1962 | 8-10 | 27.4 | 3.7 | 0.6 |
| Britain 1965-9 | 7 | 7.7 | 2.4 | 0.8 |
| | 11 | 21.2 | 3.7 | |
| Sheffield 1972 | 5-9 | | 2.95 | |
| | 10-14 | | 4.65 | |
| Camberwell 1972 (urban) | 5-9 | | 4.39 | |
| | 10-14 | | 4.17 | |
| Salford 1973 (urban) | 5-9 | | 5.73 | |
| | 10-14 | | 5.81 | |

Sources: Office of Health Economics / Jay Report

The prevalence of mental handicap is normally calculated from rates established by case studies; thus the Salford finding for 10-14 years in 1973 suggested that there were 5.81 per 1,000 population ($5.81 \times 56$ million people divided by $1{,}000 = 320{,}000$). Findings have varied due to differences in sampling, but the consensus is that the rate of mental handicap is around 20 per 1,000 and severe mental handicap around 3.2 per 1,000. This accords with findings in the 1920s suggesting no significant change although the prevalence rate for Down's is lower than current.

Table 2

**BIRTHS WITH CONGENITAL MALFORMATIONS : ENGLAND & WALES**

| | 1975 | 1976 | 1977 | 1978 | 1979 | 1980 | 1981 | 1982 | 1983 |
|---|---|---|---|---|---|---|---|---|---|
| All malformed babies | 12,230 | 12,384 | 12,402 | 12,767 | 13,529 | 14,134 | 13,450 | 13,281 | 13,972 |
| Disorders of the Central Nervous System | 2,227 | 1,915 | 1,869 | 1,757 | 1,637 | 1,476 | 1,229 | 1,016 | 917 |
| —Anencephalus | 775 | 644 | 568 | 525 | 455 | 342 | 247 | 162 | 114 |
| —Spina Bifida | 1,101 | 880 | 881 | 841 | 845 | 756 | 663 | 511 | 422 |
| —Hydrocephalus | 249 | 267 | 260 | 244 | 227 | 222 | 188 | 177 | 194 |
| —Other | 102 | 124 | 160 | 147 | 110 | 156 | 131 | 166 | 187 |
| Chromosomal | 524 | 445 | 482 | 503 | 535 | 569 | 561 | 615 | n/a |
| —Down's Syndrome | 454 | 399 | 425 | 444 | 463 | 481 | 475 | 527 | 497 |
| —Other chromosomal | 70 | 46 | 57 | 59 | 72 | 88 | 86 | 88 | n/a |

## RATES PER 1,000 BIRTHS

| | Anencephalus | Spina Bifida | Hydrocephalus | Down's Syndrome |
|---|---|---|---|---|
| 1974 | 1.31 | 1.83 | 0.48 | 0.65 |
| 1975 | 1.27 | 1.81 | 0.41 | 0.75 |
| 1976 | 1.09 | 1.49 | 0.45 | 0.68 |
| 1977 | 0.99 | 1.53 | 0.45 | 0.74 |
| 1978 | 0.87 | 1.40 | 0.41 | 0.74 |
| 1979 | 0.71 | 1.31 | 0.35 | 0.72 |
| 1980 | 0.52 | 1.14 | 0.34 | 0.73 |
| 1981 | 0.39 | 1.04 | 0.29 | 0.74 |
| 1982 | 0.26 | 0.81 | 0.28 | 0.84 |
| 1983 (Jan-June) | 0.19 | 0.71 | 0.28 | 0.86 |

Source: Office of Population Censuses and Surveys

OPCS has a monitoring service of notifications of births with congenital malformations. Out of over 13,000 births with malformations, 1,600 had disorders of the central nervous system or chromosomal abnormalities which may cause mental handicap. Trends over the last ten years show a downward movement in births with disorders such as anencephalus, spina bifida and hydrocephalus, but the incidence of chromosomal abnormalities is generally on the increase.

**Table 3**
**INFANT DEATHS AND STILLBIRTHS IN 1979 AND 1982**

| | All causes | | All congenital Anomalies | | Anencephalus | | Spina Bifida | | Other Anomalies of Central Nervous System | |
|---|---|---|---|---|---|---|---|---|---|---|
| | 1979 | 1982 | 1979 | 1982 | 1979 | 1982 | 1979 | 1982 | 1979 | 1982 |
| Stillbirths[1] | 5,125 | 3,939 | 939 | 494 | 461 | 151 | 125 | 66 | 141 | 93 |
| Perinatal[2] Deaths | 9,402 | 7,087 | 2,038 | 1,467 | 529 | 181 | 272 | 129 | 204 | 156 |
| Neonatal[3] Deaths | 5,216 | 3,925 | 1,530 | 1,282 | 69 | — | 312 | 131 | 97 | 83 |
| Postneonatal[4] Deaths | 2,848 | 2,860 | 508 | 582 | — | — | 91 | 62 | 40 | 36 |

Notes: [1]Late fetal death, after 28 weeks gestation
[2]Stillbirths and deaths in first week of life
[3]Death during first 28 days
[4]Death from 28 days to one year

Source: Mortality Statistics, OPCS

Congenital malformations associated with mental handicap are a major cause of death in the newly born and responsible for a large share of stillbirths. In terms of all congenital abnormalities, 46% die within four weeks of life, 62% by the age of one year, and 75% by the age of fifteen. Congenital anomalies are the second major cause of death among babies of under one year after perinatal causes, and the second among infants aged one and four years after accidental death.

All babies born with anencephalus die within a few weeks of life. Around 80% of spina bifida babies die within one year, and 60% of babies with congenital hydrocephalus. Roughly 40% of Down's babies have less than one year life expectancy. In all cases except anencephalus, life may continue into the 50s and 60s.

Table 3 shows that the numbers of infant deaths and stillbirths declined significantly between 1979 and 1982 due to reduced incidence of congenital anomalies.

**Table 4**
**NOTIFICATIONS OF DOWN'S SYNDROME ANALYSED BY AGE OF MOTHER, 1974-1980**
**England and Wales**

| Age of mother | 1974 | 1975 | 1976 | 1977 | 1978 | 1979 | 1980 |
|---|---|---|---|---|---|---|---|
| Numbers | | | | | | | |
| Total | 419 | 454 | 399 | 425 | 444 | 463 | 481 |
| Under 20 | 23 | 32 | 25 | 28 | 22 | 24 | 31 |
| 20-24 | 71 | 70 | 77 | 80 | 80 | 61 | 83 |
| 25-29 | 94 | 111 | 93 | 116 | 133 | 118 | 125 |
| 30-34 | 84 | 85 | 93 | 81 | 94 | 136 | 110 |
| 35-39 | 65 | 84 | 63 | 67 | 69 | 75 | 78 |
| 40-44 | 60 | 61 | 37 | 39 | 32 | 39 | 43 |
| 45 and over | 11 | 11 | 6 | 7 | 8 | 5 | 3 |
| Not stated | 11 | — | 5 | 7 | 6 | 5 | 8 |
| Rates (per 10,000 total births) | | | | | | | |
| Total | 6·5 | 7·4 | 6·8 | 7·4 | 7·4 | 7·2 | 7·3 |
| Under 20 | 3·3 | 5·0 | 4·3 | 5·1 | 3·9 | 4·0 | 5·1 |
| 20-24 | 3·4 | 3·6 | 4·2 | 4·5 | 4·3 | 3·1 | 4·1 |
| 25-29 | 4·0 | 4·9 | 4·2 | 5·5 | 6·3 | 5·3 | 5·6 |
| 30-34 | 9·3 | 9·5 | 10·1 | 8·0 | 8·2 | 10·7 | 8·4 |
| 35-39 | 21·0 | 29·3 | 23·7 | 25·9 | 24·4 | 23·6 | 22·8 |
| 40-44 | 77·9 | 89·4 | 60·1 | 69·1 | 54·8 | 63·9 | 69·6 |
| 45 and over | 193·3 | 183·9 | 116·3 | 149·6 | 150·0 | 91·6 | 46·7 |

Source: OPCS Monitor

The relationship between Down's Syndrome is well known and amply illustrated in the table above. The higher age figures show considerable fluctuations because of the smaller absolute figures involved.

**Table 5**
**MALFORMATION RATIOS BY FATHER'S SOCIAL CLASS AND MOTHER'S AGE: DOWN'S SYNDROME 1974-9**
**England and Wales**

| Father's social class | Mother's age | | | | | |
|---|---|---|---|---|---|---|
| | All ages | Under 20 | 20-24 | 25-29 | 30-34 | 35 & over |
| I-V | 100 (1,572 cases) | 48 | 51 | 73 | 134 | 502 |
| I | 118 | — | 58 | 74 | 119 | 508 |
| II | 105 | 88 | 52 | 62 | 120 | 460 |
| III N | 107 | 23 | 50 | 86 | 155 | 557 |
| III M | 90 | 58 | 54 | 68 | 118 | 456 |
| IV | 98 | 25 | 39 | 85 | 183 | 556 |
| V | 123 | 66 | 61 | 100 | 218 | 727 |

Social Classes:

| | |
|---|---|
| I | Professional occupations |
| II | Intermediate occupations |
| III N | Non-manual skilled occupations |
| III M | Manual skilled occupations |
| IV | Partly skilled |
| V | Unskilled |

Perhaps less well known is the relationship between Down's Syndrome and social class. The figures in the table are based on an index of all social classes and all age groups which equals 100 and is based on 1,572 cases. Raised ratios emerge for the social class V irrespective of the age of the mother, but social class I is also high overall because of the numbers of older mothers in this social class. The findings are still being studied but the suggestion is that younger mothers in lower social classes should be added to screening programmes.

**Table 6**
**REASONS FOR ABORTIONS AMONG MARRIED WOMEN 1974-1982**

| Reason: | 1974 | 1976 | 1978 | 1980 | 1982 |
|---|---|---|---|---|---|
| One | 687 | 529 | 410 | 380 | 394 |
| Two | 29,608 | 28,340 | 29,370 | 32,369 | 29,056 |
| Three | 13,404 | 10,405 | 10,474 | 10,051 | 9,532 |
| Four | 1,397 | 1,029 | 1,893 | 1,447 | 1,539 |
| Five | 6 | 10 | 12 | 7 | 9 |
| TOTAL | 45,102 | 40,313 | 42,159 | 44,254 | 40,510 |

Source: OPCS

### CAUSES OF ABORTIONS IN 1982

| Reason: | All | Single | Married | Widowed/ Divorced | Other |
|---|---|---|---|---|---|
| One | 655 | 189 | 374 | 77 | 15 |
| Two | 110,216 | 68,892 | 29,056 | 10,668 | 1,600 |
| Three | 15,655 | 2,424 | 9,532 | 3,450 | 259 |
| Four | 2,006 | 329 | 1,539 | 116 | 22 |
| Five | 11 | 2 | 9 | — | — |
| TOTAL | 128,553 | 71,836 | 40,510 | 14,311 | 1,896 |

Reasons: One — risk to life of mother
Two — risk to physical/mental health of mother
Three — risk to existing children
Four — substantial risk of child being mentally/physically handicapped
Five — emergency operation

Source: Abortion Statistics, OPCS

It is legal to have an abortion if there is a substantial risk of a child being born mentally or physically handicapped. Most women who have abortions for this reason are married, 77% of the total in 1982. Abortions for this reason accounted for 3.8% of all abortions among married women in 1982; there is no distinct upward or downward trend yet apparent in recorded figures.

**Table 7**
**ABORTIONS : ANALYSIS BY AGE 1980 : All Women (Married)**

| | Reason (4) | | Total | |
|---|---|---|---|---|
| Under 15 | 6 | (—) | 933 | (—) |
| 15 | 10 | (—) | 2,717 | (—) |
| 16-19 | 169 | (45) | 31,878 | (937) |
| 20-24 | 356 | (240) | 33,014 | (6,658) |
| 25-29 | 447 | (377) | 22,042 | (10,318) |
| 30-34 | 335 | (292) | 19,419 | (12,529) |
| 35-39 | 228 | (196) | 12,730 | (9,187) |
| 40-44 | 308 | (259) | 5,307 | (4,058) |
| 45 & over | 42 | (34) | 547 | (437) |
| Unknown | 5 | (4) | 340 | (121) |

Source: OPCS Abortion Statistics

England & Wales

The importance of 'Reason Four' increases significantly with the age of the mother. Of abortions among married women aged 40, over 6% were for this reason.

**Table 8**
**MEDICAL REASONS FOR ABORTIONS 1979-1982**

| England & Wales: Residents | 1979 | 1980 | 1982 |
|---|---|---|---|
| Central nervous system malformation in foetus | 285 | 418 | 486 |
| Chromosomal abnormality in foetus | 173 | 173 | 288 |
| Hereditary disease in family possibly affecting foetus | 89 | 66 | 82 |
| Suspected damage to foetus from viral disease in mother (eg rubella) | 757 | 328 | 255 |
| Damage to foetus from drugs | 254 | 298 | 310 |
| Damage to foetus from radiation | 113 | 128 | 115 |
| Other known or suspected foetal abnormality | 655 | 603 | 516 |
| Suspected damage to foetus from other disease in mother | 402 | 412 | 313 |
| TOTAL | 2,728 | 2,426 | 2,635 |

Source: Abortion Statistics, OPCS

Information on reported medical conditions for abortions suggests, however that there were more than the 2,000 abortions suggested in Table 6, and a figure of 2,700 abortions due to abnormalities would be more realistic.

## Table 9
## ABORTIONS CONCERNING MENTAL HANDICAP 1971-1977

| | 1971 | 1972 | 1973 | 1974 | 1975 | 1976 | 1977 |
|---|---|---|---|---|---|---|---|
| Malformations of central nervous system | 53 | 51 | 45 | 34 | 73 | 81 | 124 |
| Down's Syndrome | 50 | 72 | 75 | 116 | 114 | 105 | 105 |
| Other Syndromes | 1 | 3 | 1 | 3 | — | 3 | 1 |
| Multiple congenital malformations | 22 | 18 | 9 | 5 | 6 | 6 | 5 |

## Table 10
## MENTAL HANDICAP HOSPITALS IN THE UK 1961-1980

| Unit : '000s | In-patients Average daily occupied beds | In-patients discharges & deaths | Out-patients: new patients | Out-patients: attendances |
|---|---|---|---|---|
| 1961 | 53.3 | 10.4 | | |
| 1966 | 65.2 | 13.2 | 2.2 | 9.1 |
| 1971 | 64.9 | 17.6 | 3.8 | 14.4 |
| 1976 | 59.2 | 19.9 | 4.8 | 27.5 |
| 1979 | 55.4 | 25.7 | 3.2 | 23.4 |
| 1980 | 53.9 | 29.1 | 3.0 | 22.5 |
| 1981 | 52.2 | 32.8 | 3.0 | 23.8 |

Source: Social Trends

Since 1970, occupancy within mental handicap hospitals has fallen and discharges have continued to rise; attendances by new patients have also fallen away.

**Table 11**
**MENTAL HANDICAP HOSPITALS AND UNITS—ENGLAND**

| Size of Hospital or Unit | 1970 Number of Hospitals or Units | 1970 Number of Beds | 1976 Number of Hospitals or Units | 1976 Number of Beds |
|---|---|---|---|---|
| 0-49 Beds | 76 | 1,900 | 115 | 3,000 |
| 50-199 Beds | 82 | 8,600 | 88 | 9,000 |
| 200-499 Beds | 37 | 11,900 | 41 | 13,900 |
| 500-999 Beds | 23 | 15,100 | 20 | 13,000 |
| 1000-1499 Beds | 6 | 7,100 | 8 | 9,400 |
| 1500-1999 Beds | 7 | 12,300 | 3 | 4,900 |
| 2000 and Over Beds | 1 | 2,200 | — | — |
| Total | 232 | 59,200 | 275 | 53,100 |

Source: Mental Handicap : Progress, Problems and Priorities

Note: The difference between the sum of numbers of beds and the totals shown is due to rounding.

Between 1970 and 1976 the number of mental handicap hospital units increased by 20% but the average size fell from 255 beds to under 200 beds in a move to create more smaller units.

**Table 12**
**HANDICAPPED CHILDREN ATTENDING SPECIAL SCHOOLS**

at January 1983

| At Special Schools: | ESN(M) | ESN(S) | Autistic |
|---|---|---|---|
| Maintained | | | |
| —Day | 52,550 | 25,321 | 349 |
| —Boarding | 4,347 | 560 | 61 |
| Non-Maintained | | | |
| —Day | 396 | 41 | 28 |
| —Boarding | 598 | 123 | 54 |
| Special Hospital Schools | 32 | 2,207 | 97 |
| Attending Special Classes at Normal Schools[1] | 7,365 | 136 | 59 |
| Boarded in homes | 6 | 18 | — |
| Attending independent schools | 486 | 703 | 308 |
| Receiving other tuition | 239 | 422 | 23 |
| TOTAL | 66,019 | 22,531 | 979 |

[1]Excluding ESN(M) at ordinary schools
Source: Department of Education

Note: England only

At the beginning of 1983, there were 154,953 children receiving special education in England. Around 65% of these, approximately 100,000 children were being educated in special schools for the mentally handicapped. The figure of 980 children in autistic schools is under-reported.

## Table 13
## REGIONAL LOCATION OF SPECIAL SCHOOLS FOR THE MENTALLY HANDICAPPED IN ENGLAND, January 1983

| Unit: children attending[1] | ESN(M) | ESN(S) | Autistic |
|---|---|---|---|
| North | 5,093 | 2,060 | 37 |
| Yorks/Humberside | 6,976 | 2,943 | 50 |
| East Midlands | 5,887 | 2,479 | 99 |
| East Anglia | 1,927 | 1,173 | 22 |
| Greater London | 7,685 | 3,989 | 286 |
| Other South East | 16,163 | 6,619 | 211 |
| South West | 7,541 | 2,526 | 95 |
| West Midlands | 7,567 | 3,485 | 85 |
| North West | 9,497 | 4,724 | 120 |
| TOTAL ENGLAND | 68,336 | 29,998 | 1,005 |

[1]or awaiting admission
Source: Department of Education

**Table 14**
**LOCAL AUTHORITY AND VOLUNTARY PROVISION: ENGLAND & WALES**

| | 1970 | 1977 |
|---|---|---|
| Places in Local Authority Homes | | |
| —adults & children | 5,221 | 10,158 |
| —children under 16 | 1,407 | 1,721 |
| —unstaffed homes | 85 | 653 |
| Adult Training Centres | 26,649 | 40,369 |
| Special care units in Adult Training Centres | | 1,672 |
| Places in voluntary & private homes | 1,814 | 3,404 |

| (England & Wales) | 1976 | 1979 | 1980 | 1981 | 1982 |
|---|---|---|---|---|---|
| Places in Local Authority homes | 9.0 | 11.9 | 12.6 | 13.4 | 13.9 |
| Voluntary/Private homes | 3.3 | 4.0 | 4.0 | 3.1 | 4.5 |

Source: Social Trends/Jay Report

Over the period from 1970 to 1977, there was a sharp increase in local authority provision for mentally handicapped children and adults. This continued into 1982 with an increase also in voluntary and private provision.

**Table 15**
**RESIDENTIAL CARE FOR MENTALLY HANDICAPPED CHILDREN & ADULTS**
**England & Wales 1983/4 and 1984/5 estimates**

| | CHILDREN | | ADULTS | |
|---|---|---|---|---|
| | 1983/4 | 1984/5 | 1983/4 | 1984/5 |
| Number in care | 2,531 | 2,619 | 14,902 | 15,655 |
| Gross Expenditure £000 | 33,232 | 36,912 | 88,772 | 100,448 |
| Net Expenditure £000 | 30,109 | 33,313 | 63,427 | 72,332 |
| Residents' Weeks | 99,980 | 104,927 | 522,470 | 541,027 |
| % occupancy | 85 | 84 | 93 | 92 |
| Cost per resident, excl. capital charges £ | 245.2 | 267.6 | 106.3 | 114.1 |
| Inc. from charges per week | — | — | 27.8 | 29.3 |

Source: CIPFA

It is estimated that there were 14,900 adults and 2,500 children in mental handicap homes in 1983/4. The weekly cost was £106 for adults and £245 for children.

**Table 16**
**NUMBER OF REGISTERED AND UNREGISTERED MENTALLY DISABLED AND SUBNORMAL 1983**

| | TOTAL | Unemployed |
|---|---|---|
| *Registered* | | |
| Disabled | 15,875 | 5,073 |
| Mentally Handicapped & Subnormal | 13,342 | 3,708 |
| *Unregistered* | | |
| Disabled | 19,593 | |
| Mentally Handicapped & Subnormal | 10,837 | |

Source: Manpower Services Commission

# APPENDIX D:

# VOLUNTARY ORGANISATIONS CONCERNED WITH THE MENTALLY HANDICAPPED

This section lists some of the major charities and organisations in the country with direct or peripheral interests in mentally handicapped children and adults. The directorial comments are derived from a postal questionnaire conducted in 1984.

The organisations featured in this section do not necessarily endorse the views expressed in the body of this handbook, which are solely those of the author.

## ACTION RESEARCH FOR THE CRIPPLED CHILD:

The National Fund for Research into Crippling Diseases
Vincent House, North Parade, Horsham, Sussex RH12 2DA
Horsham (0403) 64101

The Fund supports research leading to the prevention of disability, especially in children, mainly concerned with physical handicap, but also multiply-handicapped children and adults with mental handicap.

*Voluntary Help* : Needed for fundraising activities

*Financial Aid* : Urgently sought to fund worthwhile research projects

The Fund operates through 1,000 local committees throughout the UK, and there are regular meetings and conferences. School talks and visits can be arranged.

**ADVISORY CENTRE FOR EDUCATION (ACE)**
18 Victoria Park Square, London E2 9PB
01-980-4596

The aim of the Centre is to press for a state-maintained education service responsive to the needs of its users. The emphasis is on disseminating information through lectures, publications and general advice services.

| | | |
|---|---|---|
| *Financial Aid* | : | As a charity, the Centre depends on grants from charitable trusts and donations are always welcome. |
| *Publications* | : | The range of publications includes the 'ACE Special Education Handbook' a detailed commentary of new legislation for children with special needs. |

A free advice service is available.

## L'ARCHE LIMITED

14 London Road, Beccles, Suffolk NR34 9NH
(0502) 715329

The aims of the organisation are to create community homes where mentally handicapped adults can live shared lives. Work projects are run in association with community homes for residents, and five communities have been established. The organisation is affiliated to the worldwide Federation of L'Arche, and the individual communities in the UK operate small, family type homes.

*Voluntary Help* : Occasional helpers required in individual localities in addition to 'live-in' volunteers receiving pocket money and lodgings.

*Financial Help* : Funds required for expansion plans for more homes in individual communities including workshops.

*Publications* : In addition to various publications describing the L'Arche concept and its activities, a quarterly magazine entitled 'Letters of L'Arche' describes the international scene. A UK newsletter is also available.

Films are available for school hire and local communities give talks on request.

## ASSOCIATION OF PARENTS OF VACCINE DAMAGED CHILDREN

2 Church Street, Shipston on Stour, Warwickshire CV36 4AP
(0608) 61595

The Association campaigns for state compensation for children injured by routine immunisation and advises parents on how to claim payment under the Vaccine Damage Payments Act 1979. It is self-financed by its members.

**ASSOCIATION OF PROFESSIONS FOR THE MENTALLY HANDICAPPED**
126 Albert Street, London NW1 7NF
01-267-6111

The Association aims to promote the general welfare of mentally handicapped people and their families by encouraging high standards of care and development and facilitating co-operation and the sharing of knowledge among those who work with them by offering a professional unified view. The Association is also keen to educate the public to accept, understand and respect mentally handicapped people.

*Voluntary Help* : Help is required for publicity and administration both nationally and with local groups.

*Financial Aid* : Funds are always required to further the aims of the Association.

*Publications* : A wide range of publications are available, mainly covering conference proceedings, project papers and workshop reports.

**ASSOCIATION FOR SPINA BIFIDA & HYDROCEPHALUS (ASBAH)**
22 Upper Woburn Place, London WC1H 0EP
01-388-1382

This association provides aid and support to children with spina bifida and/or hydrocephalus, and their families. The association provides counselling services for individual cases, and holds a bi-annual conference.

*Voluntary Help* : Voluntary helpers are needed to run independence training courses and fundraising activities

*Financial Aid* : 95% of association's funds are from voluntary contributions.

*Publications* : 'Your Child With Spina Bifida'
by J Lorber
'Your Child With Hydrocephalus'
by J Lorber
'Nursery Years'
by S Haskell & M Paull
'Children with Spina Bifida At School'
by P Henderson
'Lives in Question'
Ed ASBAH

Other publications and films are available.

**DR BARNARDO'S**

Barnardo House, Tanners Lane, Barkingside, Ilford, Essex IG6 1QG
01-550-8822

Dr Barnardo's is a national, voluntary organisation which exists to care for children in need—children who are handicapped physically, mentally, socially or emotionally. The charity runs residential homes, playschemes and a wide range of community projects including advice centres, support services for mentally handicapped children and families, fostering services and community care facilities for handicapped children previously in long-term hospitals.

*Voluntary Help* : Barnardo's require volunteers for a wide range of activities throughout the country; as helpers in their 200 gift shops, as members of 'Barnardo Helpers' for fund-raising activities and sponsored events. Other volunteers are needed to work directly with children in Barnardo's care.

*Financial Aid* : Barnardo's relies on financial donations from the public to continue its activities.

*Publications* : Several publications are available, including;
'The Open Door', a colour magazine published twice a year with a circulation of 150,000.
'Night & Day', an annual summary of the work of Dr Barnardo's for its supporters.
'Barnardo's Today', a bi-annual publication aimed at the public at large.

Counselling services are available through 'advice centres' and various back-up services are available. Barnardo's has two full-time lecturers who visit colleges and other establishments around the UK to educate the public about the charity's activities. School visits and talks can be arranged on request.

**BREAK**
20 Hooks Hill Road, Sheringham, Norfolk NR26 8NL
(0263) 823170/823025

BREAK provides short stay facilities and holidays for handicapped and deprived children and mentally and multiply handicapped adults. BREAK centres accept guests from all parts of the UK and transport facilities are available.

*Voluntary Help* : BREAK runs a year round volunteer programme, and volunteers are part of the care team sharing in rota duties in return for pocket money and lodgings.

*Financial Help* : Finance is always needed, including the creation of a holiday fund to provide free and subsidised holidays.

BREAK staff are always prepared to give school talks and two films are available.

**THE BRITISH ASSOCIATION OF ART THERAPISTS**
13c Northwood Road, London N6 5TL

BAAT exists to promote the use of Art Therapy and to promote its availability in, among other areas, special schools and hospitals. The Association acts as a professional body negotiating on behalf of art therapists and providing training courses, organising conferences, and publishing journals and newsletters on the subject.

*Publications* : 'Inscape' the journal of BAAT is published twice-yearly.

**BRITISH ASSOCIATION FOR EARLY CHILDHOOD EDUCATION**
Montgomery Hall, Kennington Oval, London SE11 5SW
01-582-8744

The Association exists to improve and maintain good standards of education for young children, disseminating research information on child development and care. The 1984 theme is special children and their educational needs.

| | |
|---|---|
| *Financial Aid* | : Funds needed to expand the activities of the Association. |
| *Publications* | : A wide range of pamphlets are available. |

Conferences, school talks and seminars are regularly conducted.

**BRITISH ASSOCIATION OF SOCIAL WORKERS**
17 Kent Street, Birmingham B5 6RD
021-622-3911

The BASW Special Interest Group is concerned with people who have mental handicap, aiming to provide the services which allow them to lead an ordinary life by all appropriate means. The establishment of services for people with a mental handicap is considered a priority within the mainstream of good social work practice. BASW also aims to provide a forum for policy attitudes and to monitor the development of social work services in this field.

Publications include the BASW position statement: 'Towards Extra Ordinary Services for People with a Mental Handicap'

BASW presents lectures and conferences on social work and mental handicap, and acts as a pressure group to develop new services.

**BRITISH EPILEPSY ASSOCIATION**
Crowthorne House, Bigshotte, New Wokingham Road, Wokingham, Berks RG11 3AY
(0344) 773122

The Association aims to increase public awareness and understanding of epilepsy through educational presentations to professional and lay audiences; provide information and advice through social work programmes and community self-help groups; and promote epilepsy research by funding research projects.

*Voluntary Help* : Help needed for local community self-help groups, and fundraising.

*Financial Aid* : Funds needed for various projects including holidays for children with severe epilepsy and research.

*Publications* : Various leaflets are available, together with a quarterly newsletter ('Epilepsy Now'), an 'Epilepsy Handbook' and other titles.

Counselling services are available at headquarters and through regional offices, and home visits can be arranged. A wide range of lectures and conferences are arranged, together with visits to schools, colleges and polytechnics.

**BRITISH INSTITUTE OF MENTAL HANDICAP**
Wolverhampton Road, Kidderminster, Worcs DY10 3PP
(0562) 850251

The BIMH aims to raise standards of treatment, care and management of mentally handicapped people both in hospital and the community, providing an information and resource centre answering enquiries on all aspects of mental handicap. Conferences and workshops are arranged on a national basis.

Publications include 'Mental Handicap', a quarterly journal covering themes in mental handicap, 'Mental Handicap Bulletin', a quarterly collection of topical articles and a monthly bibliography. Various other titles are available.

**BRITISH SOCIETY FOR MUSIC THERAPY**
Guildhall School of Music and Drama, Barbican, London EC2Y 8DT
01-368-8879

The Society aims to promote the use and development of music therapy in the treatment, education and training of children and adults with emotional, physical and mental handicaps. It holds meetings, workshops and conferences on music therapy and publishes conference papers and the 'British Journal of Music Therapy'. The Society also offers a one-year postgraduate Diploma Course in Music Therapy, and arranges counselling services, lectures and school visits on request.

**BUCKETS AND SPADES CHARITABLE TRUST**
Lancaster Road, Hollington, St Leonards on Sea, East Sussex TN38 9LX
(0424) 52119

The Trust provides short-term and holiday care for mentally handicapped children and some adults.

Funds are always needed for running the home. No statutory grant is available.

**THE CAMPAIGN FOR MENTALLY HANDICAPPED PEOPLE**
16 Fitzroy Square, London W1P 5HQ
01-387-9571

The CMH is a public education and campaigning group working to secure the rights of mentally handicapped people. It presses for services which are comprehensive and local and serve all mentally handicapped people irrespective of the severity of their disability. It works through a group of parents, professionals and friends united in their concern for mentally handicapped people, providing an information service, a contact network, regular conferences, publications, workshops and a wide range of other services.

*Financial Aid* : Funds emanate from member's subscriptions and other donations.

*Publications* : Policy and discussion papers are regularly published.

**THE CAMPHILL VILLAGE TRUST**
Delrow House, Hilfield Lane, Aldenham, Watford WD2 8DJ
Radlett (09276) 6006

A Charity providing assistance for mentally handicapped adults to move towards independence and integration within the community by providing a home, work, further education and general care. A number of communities operate throughout the country, and require voluntary helpers and staff working for pocket money and lodgings.

*Financial Aid* : Government support is available through local Social Services Departments, and other departments but additional funds are urgently required for further centres. There is currently a three-year waiting list.

Counselling services, films and school visits are available on request.

**THE CATHOLIC HANDICAPPED CHILDREN'S FELLOWSHIP**
2 The Villas, Hare Law, Stanley, Co Durham DH9 8DQ
(0207) 234379

The Fellowship provides spiritual and material welfare for the handicapped. Particular interest is taken in Catholic families.

*Voluntary Help* : All work is voluntary, and helpers needed for family care, meetings and activities for parents and the handicapped, and for weekly clubs, holidays and outings.

*Financial Aid* : Always needed.

Counselling services and school talks can be arranged on request.

**CENTRE ON ENVIRONMENT FOR THE HANDICAPPED**
126 Albert Street, London NW1 7NF
01-482-2247

CEH's main concern is to improve the environment for mentally and physically handicapped people, by making architects and other professionals better informed about special needs and the way buildings and other facilities can best serve all people. A free consultancy service is available to architects.

*Financial Aid* : The CEH undertakes specific projects for which financial support is essential.

*Publications* : Various titles available, including a 'Register of Buildings' which contains descriptions, plans and appraisals of buildings built or adapted for the needs of the mentally handicapped.

A series of twelve seminars are held each year responding to needs as identified. School visits can also be arranged.

**THE COLLEGE OF SPEECH THERAPISTS**
Harold Poster House, 6 Lechmere Road, London NW2 5BU
01-459-8521

The professional body maintaining standards of training and ethical conduct about speech therapists, and fostering research and knowledge on speech therapy. Finance is obtained through membership fees and contributions, and a range of information pamphlets are available on request.

**CONCORD FILMS COUNCIL**
201 Felixstowe Road, Ipswich, Suffolk IP3 9BJ
(0473) 76012/715754

The Council operates a 16 mm film and video cassette distribution service, distributing films and videos concerned with various contemporary social issues including mental handicap. These are made available to schools, hospitals and voluntary organisations. The Council is a self-registered charity.

A full catalogue of material available is published every two years and is available by post from the Council.

**DISABLED LIVING FOUNDATION**
546 Kensington High Street, London W14 8NS
01-602-2491

A charitable trust concerned with all aspects of ordinary life affecting people who are disabled mentally or physically. The trust operates advisory centres, an information service, a wide range of publications on all aspects of disability, counselling services, seminars on various related topics.

A recent publication, 'Give Us A Chance' discusses sport and physical recreation facilities and objectives for mentally handicapped people.

*Financial Aid* : As a charity, funding is always sought.

**DOWN'S CHILDREN ASSOCIATION**
4 Oxford Street, London W1N 9FL
01-580-0511/2

The DCA provides information to parents and others about the care of people with Down's Syndrome, encourages and publishes research work, and arranges meetings and discussions on the subject.

*Voluntary Help* : Help is required to establish a national Resource Centre to cover all aspects of mental handicap, linked to research being carried out at the National Centre for Down's Syndrome in Birmingham.

*Financial Aid* : Funding is also required for the above.

*Publications* : Range of titles including:
'Down's Syndrome. Let's Be Positive'
by J R Ludlow
'The Genetics of Down's Syndrome—An Account for Parents'
by M d'A Crawford

Other titles are available both published by the DCA or available from their bookshop, or by post.

The DCA provides contact addresses throughout the country for counselling, usually parents of children with Down's Syndrome. Branches of the Association throughout the country hold regular meetings and Conferences are organised twice-yearly. A panel of speakers are available for visits and lectures.

**THE FAMILY FUND**
PO Box 50, York YO1 1UY
(0904) 21115

This is a government fund administered by the Joseph Rowntree Memorial Trust to help families with very severely handicapped children under 16 years of age. Help given includes family holidays and outings and various practical forms of help as a complement to existing services.

**FAMILY PLANNING ASSOCIATION EDUCATION UNIT**
27-35 Mortimer Street, London W1N 7RJ
01-631-0555

The FPA is a professional training, education and consultation service on all aspects of personal relationships and sex education. It runs courses in personal relationships and sexuality for a wide range of professionals, including teachers, youth workers, social workers and nurses. Recently, a large number of courses have been for staff working with mentally handicapped people.

*Financial Aid* : Courses are generally funded by government departments but new developments such as courses for parents require additional financial support.

Counselling services are available through the FPA's information department.

**THE GUARDIANSHIP SOCIETY**
Eyre Woodhead Memorial, Corner Avondale Road, Old Shoreham Road, Hove, BN3 6EW
Brighton 739887

The Society has 310 mentally handicapped adults in its care, and arranges to foster children and adults with suitable parents. It operates three training centres, providing occupational therapy plus social training. The overall aims are to integrate mentally handicapped people into the community and assist them to lead as normal a life as their handicap allows.

*Voluntary Help* : Mainly transport requirements.

*Financial Aid* : General funds always sought for improvements to facilities.

**THE HANDICAPPED ADVENTURE PLAYGROUND ASSOCIATION LIMITED**
Fulham Palace, Bishops Avenue, London SW6 6EA
01-736-4443

The Association makes provision through the medium of play for children and young people with all types of handicap. It establishes and maintains adventure playgrounds especially designed for the handicapped.

| | | |
|---|---|---|
| *Voluntary Help* | : | The charity is run by volunteers, and helpers are needed for management and office work, the charity shop, fundraising and additional play support on the five playgrounds. |
| *Financial Aid* | : | Always needed, for staff wages and their information and advisory service, and repair and building work on the sites. |
| *Publications* | : | 'Starting an Adventure Playground for Handicapped Children', an information pack, and 'Adventure Playgrounds for Handicapped Children', a booklet. |

The Association is pleased to provide advice to others wishing to set up similar projects.

**HESTAIR ADRIAN RESEARCH CENTRE**
The University, Manchester M13 9PL
061-273-3333

The Centre is involved in research projects for the study of learning processes in the mentally handicapped.

**HOME FARM TRUST LIMITED**
43-45 Queens Road, Clifton, Bristol
(0272) 23746

The Trust operates nine homes nationally for 270 residents providing whole life, residential care, together with short term respite care, day care facilities and assessment services.

| | | |
|---|---|---|
| *Voluntary Help* | : | Required for staffing and fundraising. |
| *Financial Aid* | : | Required for capital development (£1 million per new house) and various ongoing projects. |
| *Publications* | : | A yearbook describing the Trust's activities is available. |

The Trust offers counselling services to the parents and families on its waiting list, which number some 1,500, and will arrange schools talks and visits describing their aims and objectives.

**HYPERACTIVE CHILDREN'S SUPPORT GROUP**
59 Meadowside, Angmering, Sussex
Littlehampton 25182

The Group provides support for parents with hyperactive children in the form of counselling, information and notions to bring relief and help parents to cope with their children's hyperactivity. It is involved also in research work into the causes of hyperactivity and its prevention.

*Voluntary Help* : People are needed to help parents of hyperactive children with respite care and help round the home.

*Financial Aid* : The Group survives on voluntary donations and subscriptions as it receives no grants—hyperactivity is not fully recognised by the DHSS.

*Publications* : 'A Lack of Essential Fatty Acids as a Possible Cause of Hyperactivity'
'Help for Hyperactive Children' (includes details of the Feingold Food Programme)

The Group runs training courses and conferences and will give school talks and visits where possible.

**INTERNATIONAL VOLUNTARY SERVICE**
Ceresole House, 53 Regent Road, Leicester L61 6YL
0533 541862

The IVS brings together people from different nationalities and backgrounds to undertake voluntary work projects for the benefit of the community. These include some projects for mentally handicapped people.

**IN TOUCH**
10 Norman Road, Sale, Cheshire M33 3DF
061-962-4441

A contacts and information service basically for mental handicap but increasingly catering for rare physical disorders in children. The service is personal and advice/information is available to parents and professionals on behalf of parents. The organisation searches out contacts for parents whose children have rare disorders and circulates members' views and queries in a newsletter published three times each year.

*Financial Aid* : Mainly obtained through members' contributions, but any parent may use the services. Additional funding is always sought.

*Publications* : 'Coming to Terms with Mental Handicap' by Ann Worthington
'Useful Addresses for Parents with a Handicapped Child' by Ann Worthington
'Glossary of Terms—Mental Handicap and Allied Disorders' by Ann Worthington

The information service is available to anyone with a relevant enquiry and occasional talks can be arranged on request.

**INVALID CHILDREN'S AID ASSOCIATION (ICAA)**
126 Buckingham Palace Road, London SW1W 9SB
01-730-9891/6

The association runs four residential special schools for the mentally handicapped, including one for senior age boys with severe asthma/eczema and allied conditions, and three for children with specific speech and language disorders. It also operates a social work service covering parts of Greater London and Surrey, which offers help and support to families with handicapped children. An information service is available.

*Voluntary Help* : Voluntary help is required for a wide range of activities.

*Financial Aid* : The association welcomes financial support. At present, funds are required to build extensions to existing school facilities, and develop research and social work facilities in all areas of activity.

*Publications* : Range of publications available, with particular emphasis on language therapy;
'Language Through Reading', a structured scheme for teaching language for children with language learning difficulties.
'ICAA List of Educational Provision for Children with Speech and Language Disorders', a reference book containing details of Local Authority and Voluntary Organisation provision.
'ICAA Speech and Language Disorders Newsletter', news, views and developments in the field of speech and language disorder.

**JEWISH SOCIETY FOR THE MENTALLY HANDICAPPED**
Stanmore Cottage, Old Church Lane, Stanmore, Middlesex HA7 1DD
01-954 0257/1663

The Society liaises with Local Authorities for the improvement of existing and the establishment of new curative educational and training centres; encourages the extension of special care facilities at existing Jewish schools, and provides a social welfare and counselling advisory service for Jewish families.

*Voluntary Help* : Help is required for integrated youth activities, welfare visits, office and transport.

*Financial Aid* : Finance is required for workshops, residential homes, social education centres, short term care projects and holiday programmes.

*Publications* : The Society has a newsletter published three times per month, an information booklet, and 'Shabbot', a booklet for children.

This is a parent-supported group with about 300 members and 200 associates. Services are available to people of any religion, and include counselling services by social workers and welfare teams, and general advice and support. Two to three seminars are organised each year, and school visits and talks are available on request.

**KIDS**
80 Waynflete Square, London W10 6UD
01-969-2817

A home-based learning service which offers a systematic approach in helping young children to learn at home, closely involving parents; developmental play sessions for pre-school children; holiday play-schemes for physically vulnerable children; training towards independence for adolescents with special needs; counselling for parents of newly handicapped children; outings and activities for brothers and sisters of handicapped children; regular meetings, discussions and films for parents; a daily information and advice service, and a book and toy lending scheme.

*Voluntary Help* : Required for playschemes.

*Financial Aid* : Always needed.

**KING'S FUND CENTRE**
126 Albert Street, London NW1 7NF
01-267-6111

The Centre's chief aims are to provide a forum for discussion and study to accelerate the introduction of new ideas and practice in the planning and management of health and social services, including those relevant to the care and treatment of mental handicap. The Long Term Care Team aims to develop better services for the mentally ill, mentally handicapped, elderly and disabled.

The Centre has a library and information services system including much information on mental handicap. It is open 9.30am to 5.30pm Mondays to Saturdays inclusive and is open to the public.

The Centre organises various conferences and has an extensive publications list.

**MACINTYRE SCHOOLS LIMITED**
2 Ridgeway Court, Grovebury Road, Leighton Buzzard, Beds LU7 8SW
0525-370102

Macintyre provides education, training, therapeutic treatment and life-time care as appropriate for mentally handicapped children and adults. It now operates two schools with 106 residents.

*Voluntary Help* : Committed help needed in the running of the schools, and general activities such as fund-raising.

*Financial Aid* : Macintyre is a registered charity and therefore dependent on financial support to develop its facilities.

**MEDIC-ALERT FOUNDATION**
11/13 Clifton Terrace, London N4 3JP
01-263-8597

Medic-Alert provides special bracelets and pendants which will give immediate help to police, ambulance and medical services warning of hidden allergies, or particular conditions such as epilepsy, which may be present in accident victims. The emblems may be worn by mentally handicapped children requiring special medical treatment if lost.

On the reverse of the emblems are details of the patient's condition and a 24-hour telephone number for further details and contact.

Medic-Alert is a worldwide non-profit making registered charity in constant need of financial support.

**THE MENTAL HEALTH FOUNDATION**
8 Hallam Street, London W1N 6DH
01-580-0145/6

The Foundation is Britain's leading grant-making charity concerned with promoting, encouraging and financing pioneering research and community care projects in the field of mental health and mental disorder.

*Voluntary Help* : Fundraising activities.

*Financial Aid* : The Foundation is dependent on voluntary contributions to fund research and general projects.

*Publications* : 'Someone to Talk to' a directory of self-help groups and support services in the community.

The Foundation holds conferences and can arrange school/college visits.

**NATIONAL ASSOCIATION OF MENTAL HEALTH (MIND)**
22 Harley Street, London W1N 2ED
01-637-0741

MIND is the leading mental health organisation in England and Wales. Its goal is to improve and develop services for people who are mentally ill or mentally handicapped, and to encourage discussion of mental health issues in the community. To achieve this, it operates as a focus of information and expertise on all aspects of mental health.

The organisation has 160 affiliated local groups, six regional resource centres and a head office in Central London.

MIND is primarily concerned with mental illness rather than mental handicap but remains a strong pressure group for the rights of the mentally handicapped, in particular their legal rights. The organisation has also campaigned actively against children remaining in mental hospitals.

*Voluntary Help* : Volunteers are always sought for MIND's regional branches.

*Financial Aid* : Despite a government grant, funding is urgently sought for the organisation's wide ranging activities.

*Publications* : An extensive range of publications are available on mental illness and mental handicap. Titles on mental handicap include:
'Parents and Mentally Handicapped Children' by Charles Hannam
'Getting Together—Sexual and Social Expression for Mentally Handicapped People'
'Services for Mentally Handicapped People'.

## THE NATIONAL AUTISTIC SOCIETY

276 Willesden Lane, London NW2 5AL
01-451-3844

The Society provides day and residential centres for the care and education of autistic children, assisting and counselling parents, fostering research into autism and increasing awareness among the general public. The Society owns and manages six schools, an adult community, a hostel and a day centre.

| | | |
|---|---|---|
| *Voluntary Help* | : | Individual schools and centres require voluntary helpers for play activities and general support. |
| *Financial Aid* | : | The Society receives no public funds so is dependent on voluntary contributions. Projects currently in need of support include extensions to existing schools and the opening of a new school in Devon. |
| *Publications* | : | A wide range of titles mainly about autism are available through the Society's office or by post, including a number of papers by Lorna Wing. |

The Society also offers an information and advisory service for parents and professionals and runs regular conferences. School visits can be arranged through local schools.

**NATIONAL COUNCIL FOR SPECIAL EDUCATION**
1 Wood Street, Stratford upon Avon, Warwickshire CV37 6JE
0789-205332

The aims of the Council are to promote the education, training, treatment, rehabilitation and advancement of all handicapped infants, children and adults impaired by emotional, visual, physical or mental handicap. Activities include a range of publications, lectures, conferences and courses on these issues.

*Voluntary Help* : Voluntary help requirements are furnished by the members and supporters of the Council.

*Financial Aid* : As a voluntary organisation, financial aid is always sought for a wide range of research projects.

*Publications* : The NCSE publishes a quarterly journal entitled 'Special Education: Forward Trends' and aimed at all those concerned with the education of children with special educational needs. Other publications are aimed at teachers, a termly newsletter for members, and the 'NCSE Research Exchange', a focus on research with practical implications.

An information and counselling service is available through the Information Officer, Mr Roger Grimsley, 4 Julian Way, Kingsthorpe, Northampton. An annual conference is held in April each year and branches can provide speakers for school talks if required.

**NATIONAL COUNCIL FOR VOLUNTARY ORGANISATIONS**
26 Bedford Square, London WC1B 3HU
01-636-4066

The NCVO publishes a comprehensive directory of voluntary organisations covering over 600 organisations, including organisations concerned with mental handicap. The directory is available from booksellers or the above address.

**THE NATIONAL DEAF CHILDREN'S SOCIETY**
45 Hereford Road, London W2 5AH
01-229-9272/4

This is the only charity which exists specifically to represent the national interests of deaf children, provide a wide range of information and counselling services, talks, visits and conferences. Although deafness is not a mental handicap, the Society provides support to multiply handicapped deaf children and their families.

## NATIONAL FEDERATION OF GATEWAY CLUBS

117 Golden Lane, London EC1Y 0RT
01-253-9433

Gateway clubs are affiliated to Mencap and provide the most wide-ranging and substantial provision of leisure and social facilities for the mentally handicapped in the UK.

The objectives of Gateway may be summarised as follows:

(1) the provision of opportunities for the enjoyment of facilities for leisure and recreation,
(2) the organisation of a programme of activities both within and without the club which will promote the emotional development and social adjustment of the members,
(3) the provision of facilities for the continuing physical and mental development of the members,
(4) through such activities as the Gateway Award Scheme the development of personal characteristics of perseverance and initiative as a means of developing self-confidence and independence of family approval and support, and
(5) the education of society generally in an understanding of the needs of the mentally handicapped, especially that of acceptance into the community.

Gateway runs 600 affiliated clubs in England, Northern Ireland and Wales, providing leisure facilities for 38,000 members through the involvement of 18,000 volunteers. The local clubs operate weekly or bi-weekly social/pastime meetings, day trips and outings and in some cases holidays for the mentally handicapped.

*Voluntary Help* : Gateway clubs are the most practical and immediate way that people can mix with and help the mentally handicapped people in society. Clubs operate in most towns and are in constant need of volunteers to involve themselves with the clubs' activities.

*Financial Aid* : Gateway receives a grant from the Department of Education and Science but is in constant need of further funding within the auspices of the broader efforts of Mencap.

**ROYAL SOCIETY FOR MENTALLY HANDICAPPED CHILDREN AND ADULTS (MENCAP)**
Mencap National Centre, 123 Golden Lane, London EC1Y 0RT
01-253-9433

MENCAP is the largest national parent organisation in Britain providing services for mentally handicapped people and their families. It was founded in 1946, and now comprises of 55,000 members with a constantly expanding range of services provided through 12 regional offices and over 500 local societies and affiliated groups.

MENCAP runs an extensive range of services on behalf of the mentally handicapped, including counselling services, babysitting services, and holiday and hostel facilities for parents. It operates residential homes for the mentally handicapped, Gateway clubs offering nationwide social facilities, a comprehensive national scheme of holidays for the mentally handicapped, and welfare, legal and counselling services for all involved with mental handicap. The London office has a comprehensive bookshop and information service on all aspects of mental handicap.

MENCAP further operates an education training and employment service providing day release courses and seminars for staff employed in mental handicap services. Its marketing and communications department organises appeals and publicises the aims and activities of the organisation.

*Voluntary Help* : Mencap has a trained staff of 400 but essentially depends on volunteers to support and expand its nationwide activities. These include volunteers on Mencap holidays and at Gateway clubs, help with local charity shops, local fundraising and many other activities. Local societies throughout the country mainly comprise of voluntary helpers.

*Financial Aid* : Mencap is the leading charity working on behalf of the mentally handicapped in Britain today. Financial aid is constantly sought to develop the charity's activities in this field.

*Publications* : Mencap publish a wide range of books and pamphlets on all aspects of mental handicap. A full list of publications is available on request.

Mencap has counselling services, and will arrange school talks and visits on request, either through the central or local departments.

The organisation summarised its needs and aims in its 1983 Annual Report:

"MENCAP has a wide range of schemes and projects. Many rely to a large extent on volunteers and this is the most obvious way to help. Some projects need trained people, some provide training and some need the kind of help good neighbours already provide.

Many families simply appreciate a little day-to-day help. There may be mothers who need a 'sitter' to allow them to shop, to have a hairdressing appointment or to make a visit to family friends.

Transport is often a real problem; help in getting to medical or other appointments, to main-line stations for holidays or to evening meetings will be greatly appreciated. Driving parents to visit their children in residential schools or hospitals also gives them the chance to meet more often.

For those with special skills, the leisure programmes provided by Gateway Clubs can always make use of people willing to help mentally handicapped people to make music, to paint or make models, to learn dances, improve games skills or swimming.

You can help to raise funds, locally, by supporting activities advertised in your local press, by buying—and selling—our Christmas cards, which provide annually a large part of the financial support to Local Societies.

Those who wish to make a direct financial contribution may care to covenant a donation to the Society, or even to bequeath money in a will.

There is also something even more important than time or money, and yet much easier to give. If you really want to help mentally handicapped people, smile when you meet a handicapped person in the street, have a friendly word when you see them on buses and trains, don't rush to help with things they can easily do for themselves. In other words, treat them like other people. Mentally handicapped people want to live and be accepted in the community just like the rest of us; with a little help, they will be."

**NATIONAL SOCIETY FOR PREVENTION OF CRUELTY TO CHILDREN**
67 Saffron Hill, London EC1N 8RS
01-242-1625

The Society provides a 24-hour service to children and families throughout the UK investigating, assessing and treating child abuse.

| | | |
|---|---|---|
| *Voluntary Help* | : | Required for fundraising and various other activities. |
| *Financial Aid* | : | Funds sought for many projects in the Society's centenary year. |
| *Publications* | : | Wide range of titles available. |

The Society's training department provides a range of short courses on child abuse and a network of school organisers will provide school talks.

**PARENTS FOR CHILDREN**
222 Camden High Street, London NW1 8QR
01-485 7526/7548

The organisation aims to provide a permanent family placement, usually by adoption, for mentally or physically handicapped children.

*Financial Aid* : As a registered charity with some government funding, additional finance is required for special projects and a trust fund for individual families and parents.

*Voluntary Help* : Needed for relief work with parents and befriending children.

Counselling services, lectures and school visits can all be arranged on the subject of adoption. The organisation welcomes enquiries from people interested in adopting a handicapped child within 100 miles of London.

**PLAY MATTERS/**
**NATIONAL TOY LIBRARIES ASSOCIATION**
Seabrook House, Darkes Lane, Potters Bar, Herts EN6 2HL
Potters Bar (0707) 44571

The Association aims to encourage and support the development of toy libraries for all children and people with special needs, through the provision of advice, information and training. In particular, the Association advises on toys and play activities suitable for children with special needs.

*Voluntary Help* : Individual, autonomous toy libraries use helpers for toy library sessions, transport, making and repairing toys and general fundraising. Play Matters prepares an annual programme of work and raises funds for its implementation.

*Publications* : 'The Good Toy Guide', an annual publication listing all toys tested and recommended, highlighting toys suitable for people with special needs. A range of other booklets on aspects of play for special children are also available, and 'Active Worksheets' give instructions for making play and leisure aids for severely disabled people.

Individual toy libraries are available for school talks.

**PRE-SCHOOL PLAYGROUPS ASSOCIATION**
Alford House, Aveline Street, London SE11 5DH
01-582-8871

The PPA exists to help parents to provide for the needs of very young children through a voluntary network of mother and toddler groups, playgroups, and the families of the under-fives who attend them. It is an educational charity with playgroups serving half a million children. There are 400 local branches. The Association believes that all children have a right to stimulating play in the company of other children and therefore welcomes families with small handicapped children.

*Voluntary Help* : Helpers are needed for the local playgroups.

*Financial Aid* : Various projects are always in hand requiring funding.

*Publications* : Many publications are available on playgrounds, play groups, and play activities. Details from the PPA.

The PPA organises courses and conferences and will arrange school visits through local branches.

**THE RAVENSWOOD FOUNDATION**
Adastra House, 401/405 Nether Street, Finchley Central, London N3 1QG
01-346-8631/3

The Foundation operates Ravenswood Village, a residential unit for mentally handicapped children and young adults with chalets, a school, a day care unit, an adult centre and various other related services and facilities. The centre can provide short and long term care and educational training.

**RETARDED CHILDREN'S AID SOCIETY/
PETER PAN HOMES**
2 Warwick Road, New Barnet, Herts
01-441-2988

The Society operates homes in the community for mentally handicapped people, and offers holiday facilities.

As a registered charity, funds and contributions are always needed.

**RIDING FOR THE DISABLED ASSOCIATION**
Avenue 'R', National Agricultural Centre, Kenilworth, Warwickshire CV8 2LY
(0203) 56107

The Association provides opportunities for disabled and mentally handicapped people to learn to ride, operating 590 member groups throughout the United Kingdom. The Association is organised into 18 geographical regions.

*Voluntary Help* : Helpers needed at each local centre.

*Financial Aid* : Required for new special purpose centres.

*Publications* : Handbooks and newsletters are available.

Lectures are conducted at local centres and school visits can be organised through such groups.

**THE ROYAL ASSOCIATION IN AID OF THE DEAF
AND DUMB**
27 Old Oak Road, Acton, London W3 7HN
01-743-6187

RADD provides a direct service of communications with, and interpretation for, profoundly deaf and blind/deaf people. Among these are mentally handicapped people with sense impairments.

**ROYAL NATIONAL INSTITUTE FOR THE BLIND**
224 Great Portland Street, London W1N 6AA
01-388-1266

The Institute provides a wide range of services for the blind, of which a small proportion are mentally handicapped.

Comprehensive services are available providing publications, lectures, conferences, and counselling services, and voluntary and financial help is always needed.

**THE SAVE THE CHILDREN FUND**
Mary Datchelor House, 17 Grove Lane, Camberwell, London SE5 8RD
01-703-5400

An international organisation wholly concerned with the rescue in disaster and long term welfare of children in hunger, sickness and need which in the UK takes the form of family centres, hospital playschemes and work with young offenders. The Fund has a programme with handicapped children, operating playschemes at mentally handicapped hospitals. It also runs Playtrac, a travelling advice and teaching centre on play for mentally handicapped children.

*Voluntary Help* : Help is welcomed in the playschemes for mentally handicapped children and others with special needs.

*Financial Aid* : Funds are much needed for a wide range of projects many involving mentally handicapped children. These would focus on providing play and short term care facilities for children in residential and foster homes.

## SCOTTISH SOCIETY FOR THE MENTALLY HANDICAPPED

13 Elmbank Street, Glasgow G2 4QA
041-226-4541

This is a parent-based organisation concerned with all aspects of the welfare of mentally handicapped people in Scotland. It aims to achieve better services for mentally handicapped people by presenting their needs to the authorities responsible for meeting them. It provides a range of voluntary activities to complement this, including social and recreational clubs, holiday facilities and parents meetings. Current projects include a development project in Glasgow for the profoundly handicapped.

*Voluntary Help* : The Society has 80 branches which rely on volunteers for all aspects of their work, including the running of clubs and holidays.

*Financial Aid* : The Society has a wide range of needs dependent on public support.

*Publications* : 'News-Link', a periodic magazine, leaflets and occasional books.

Counselling is organised on an informal basis through branches and lectures and school visits can be organised on request.

The Society has established the Key Housing Association which is active in providing housing for the mentally handicapped.

**SENSE: THE NATIONAL DEAF, BLIND AND RUBELLA ASSOCIATION**
311 Grays Inn Road, London WC1X 8PT
01-278-1000

SENSE provides a range of services and advice for families with deaf-blind children, operates a further education centre for deaf-blind young adults and a pre-school service for young deaf-blind children. It campaigns for increased vaccination against rubella, still a major cause of mental handicap.

*Voluntary Help* : Regular holidays rely on volunteer help, whilst the two centres welcome support.

*Financial Aid* : Funds needed for new centres and developments.

**SESAME**
Christchurch, 27 Blackfriars Road, London SE1 8NY
01-633-9690

SESAME exists to explore and promote the use of movement and simple forms of drama as a therapy for the mentally or physically handicapped and ill as part of a total treatment plan. Its work includes the provision of direct patient services, the training of new practitioners specialising in this form of treatment and the teaching of special skills to staff engaged in the care of patients. Activities are offered to children and adults in special centres and in the community.

*Voluntary Help* : Mainly for fundraising.

*Financial Aid* : Always required.

SESAME speakers can be provided for seminars and conferences and workshops can be organised on request. School talks can also be arranged.

A newsletter and various films are available.

**SOCIAL CARE ASSOCIATION**
23a Victoria Road, Surbiton, Surrey KT6 4JZ
01-390-6831

The aims of the Association are to promote and encourage a high standard of service for people receiving residential and day care, and high standards of training and professional practice. The Association also represents the views of its members on matters of residential and day care and publishes magazines and other publications to this intent.

The Association holds 10-12 seminars per year, and arranges visits and talks at places of further education.

*Publications* : 'Giving Our Best' a collection of articles examining current thinking, development and practice in residential and day care
(Ed J Hyland & C Pragnell)
'Caring For Deprived Children' International case studies
(Ed C J Payne & K White)
'Why Care' Articles on values underlying residential work
(Ed D Lane & K White)
'A Way of Life for the Handicapped'
(Ed N Tutt, G Jones)
Others.

**THE SONS OF DIVINE PROVIDENCE**

25 Lower Teddington Road, Kingston upon Thames, London KT1 4HB
01-977-5130

The charity operates three homes for the mentally handicapped as part of an international organisation of care, providing residential and short term care facilities. The Sons of Divine Providence are a Catholic order.

*Voluntary Help* : Helpers are needed at the homes and for general fundraising.

*Financial Aid* : Needed for new homes.

*Publications* : 'The Bridge', a quarterly magazine.

Counselling services and school visits can be arranged on request.

**THE SPASTICS SOCIETY**
12 Park Crescent, London W1N 4EQ
01-636-5020

The Society is concerned with all aspects of the education, care, assessment, and training of people with cerebral palsy. It also provides a range of social services, campaigns on issues relating to disability and funds research into the causes and treatment of cerebral palsy and spasticity.

Counselling services are available through the Fitzroy Family Services & Assessment Centre, 16 Fitzroy Square, London W1. The Society also organises numerous conferences and talks and school visits can be organised with the regional officers in nearly 200 local groups affiliated to the Society.

*Voluntary Help* : Volunteers are needed for a wide range of activities run by the local groups.

*Financial Aid* : As a charity, the Society is dependent on popular support.

*Publications* : 'Disability Now' a monthly newsletter with free circulation.

**THE VOLUNTEER CENTRE**
29 Lower King's Road, Berkhamsted, Herts HP4 2AB
(04427) 73311

The purpose of the Centre is to encourage voluntary action in the services provided for the community by government and independent organisations, incorporating all areas of voluntary activity including needs within the field of mental handicap. It is a national advisory agency with services available to statutory and voluntary organisations, small groups and central/local government. It disseminates information on voluntary action, provides training for people managing volunteers, and services a nationwide network of volunteer bureaux. A wide range of publications is available on request.